Stitch by Stitch

Volume 2

TORSTAR BOOKS

NEW YORK · TORONTO

Stitch by Stitch

TORSTAR BOOKS INC.
300 E. 42ND STREET,
NEW YORK, NY 10017

Knitting and crochet abbreviations

approx = approximately
beg = begin(ning)
ch = chain(s)
cm = centimeter(s)
cont = continue(ing)
dc = double crochet
dec = decreas(e)(ing)
dtr = double triple
foll = follow(ing)
g = gram(s)
grp = group(s)
hdc = half double
  crochet

in = inch(es)
inc = increas(e)(ing)
K = knit
oz = ounce(s)
P = purl
patt = pattern
psso = pass slipped
  stitch over
rem = remain(ing)
rep = repeat
RS = right side
sc = single crochet
sl = slip

sl st = slip stitch
sp = space(s)
st(s) = stitch(es)
tbl = through back of
  loop(s)
tog = together
tr = triple crochet
WS = wrong side
wyib = with yarn in
  back
wyif = with yarn in front
yd = yard(s)
yo = yarn over

A guide to the pattern sizes

		10	12	14	16	18	20
Bust	in	32½	34	36	38	40	42
	cm	83	87	92	97	102	107
Waist	in	25	26½	28	30	32	34
	cm	64	67	71	76	81	87
Hips	in	34½	36	38	40	42	44
	cm	88	92	97	102	107	112

Torstar Books also offers a range of acrylic book stands, designed to keep instructional books such as *Stitch by Stitch* open, flat and upright while leaving the hands free for practical work.

For information write to Torstar Books Inc., 300 E.42nd Street, New York, NY 10017.

Library of Congress Cataloging in Publication Data
Main entry under title:

Stitch by stitch.

Includes index.
1. Needlework. I. Torstar Books (Firm)
TT705.S74 1984   746.4   84-111
ISBN 0-920269-00-1 (set)

987654

© Marshall Cavendish Limited 1985

Printed in Belgium

ISBN 0-920269-02-8 (Volume 2)

Step-by-Step Crochet Course

Step-by-Step Knitting Course

Contents

Crochet / COURSE 6

*Shaping with single
 crochet and half doubles
*Working a slip stitch
*Three smock patterns
 for babies

Shaping with single crochet and half doubles

Because of the height of most crochet stitches, it is important to be careful when increasing or decreasing a stitch at the fabric edge so the edge will be straight and smooth. A single error at the beginning or end of a row when you are decreasing will produce a stepped edge that is not only unattractive, but also difficult to sew up. This happens particularly when working with half doubles. To avoid it, a single stitch is usually decreased by working two stitches together, one stitch in from the edge. Increase one stitch on the second and next-to-last second stitches in a row to get a really smooth edge.

To decrease one single crochet at each end of a row

1 Work 1 turning chain at the beginning of the row and skip the first stitch in the usual way.

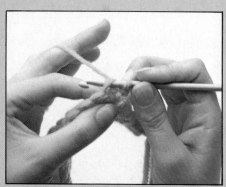

2 Insert hook from front to back into next stitch.

3 Wind yarn clockwise around hook and draw through a loop—2 loops on hook.

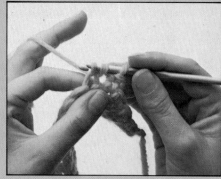

4 Insert hook into next stitch. Wind yarn clockwise around hook and draw through a loop—3 loops on hook.

5 Wind yarn around hook and draw through all 3 loops on hook—1 stitch decreased.

6 Work in single crochet to last 3 stitches.

7 Work the next 2 stitches together by repeating steps 2 to 5.

8 Work the last stitch into the turning chain of the previous row.

To decrease one half double at each end of a row

1 Work 2 turning chains at the beginning of the row and skip the first stitch in the usual way.

2 Wind yarn around hook and insert hook into next stitch.

3 Wind yarn around hook and draw through a loop—3 loops on hook.

4 Wind yarn around hook. Insert hook into next stitch.

5 Wind yarn around hook and draw through a loop—5 loops on hook.

6 Wind yarn around hook and draw through all 5 loops on hook—1 stitch decreased.

7 Work 1 half double into each stitch to last 3 stitches.

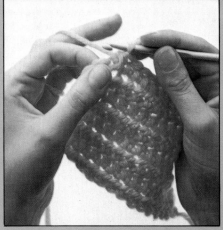

8 Work next 2 stitches together by repeating steps 2 to 6.

9 Work the last half double into the turning chain of the previous row. One stitch has been decreased at each end of row.

To increase one single crochet or one half double at each end of a row

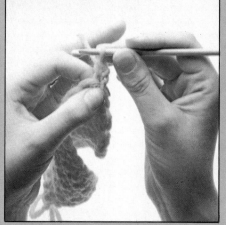

1 Work the turning chain at the beginning of the row in the usual way.

2 Skip first single crochet, work 2 single crochets into the 2nd stitch of the previous row.

3 Continue to work into each stitch to the last 2 single crochets.

4 Work 2 single crochets into the next stitch.

5 Work the last single crochet into the turning chain of the previous row. One stitch has been increased at each end.

6 Work in exactly the same way for half doubles.

Working a slip stitch

It is possible to use crochet slip stitch in various ways, but the working method is always the same. Use it as a means of shaping: either by working over several stitches at the beginning of a row to decrease them, or as a means of getting from one point to another in a row (as when making buttonholes or shaping a neck).

Slip stitch can also be used to join the two ends of a round when working circular motifs.

Slip stitch is seldom used by itself in a pattern, except when making a crochet cord. The shallowness of the stitch produces a firm cord, which is often used for ties on baby clothes.

To make a crochet cord

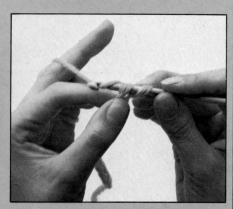

1 Make the length of chain you need. Insert the hook from front to back into the 2nd chain from hook.

2 Wind the yarn clockwise around the hook.

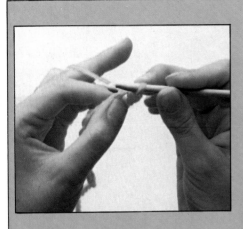

3 Draw a loop through both loops on the hook. One slip stitch made.

4 Work 1 slip stitch into each chain to the end to make the cord.

5 To make a firmer cord with a braided look, work 1 slip stitch into each chain along the other side.

Three baby smocks

Three pretty variations on the smock theme; one with sleeves, two without, worked in single crochet and doubles. Made in a fine, soft yarn, they are either solid or striped, with easy shaping on the skirt.

Baby's smock with sleeves

Size
To fit a baby up to 6 months old.
Length from shoulder, 11¼in (28.5cm) excluding contrast edging.
Sleeve seam, 6in·(15cm).

Materials
4oz (100g) of a baby yarn
Small quantity of a contrasting color for edging and back ties
No. 4 steel (1.75mm) crochet hook
No. 0 steel (2.00mm) crochet hook
Note: To make the striped smock, work every two rows in a contrasting color.

Gauge
24 stitches and 12 rows to 4in (10cm) over doubles on a No. 4 steel (1.75mm) hook.

To make smock front
Using No. 4 steel (1.75mm) hook chain 58. Work 1 double into 4th chain from hook, 1 double into each chain to end. Turn. 56 stitches.
□ Work 20 rows of doubles, increasing 1 stitch at each end of every row by working 1 stitch into the first stitch after the turning chain instead of skipping it at the beginning of the row and 2 stitches into the 2nd to last stitch at the end of the row. The skirt will measure approximately 7in (17.5cm) and there will be a total of 96 stitches in all.
Draw yarn through last loop and fasten off.

To make bodice
Return to chain at beginning of skirt. Skip first 7 chains for armhole. With right side facing, using No. 0 steel (2.00mm) hook, rejoin yarn to the 8th chain and work a row of single crochet across the chain, working the last single crochet into the 8th chain from the end, leaving the last 7 chains for the second armhole.
□ Continue working in single crochet on these 44 stitches for 2⅜in (6cm).

To shape neck
Work across first 16 single crochets on next row, then turn and work on these stitches only for one side of neck.

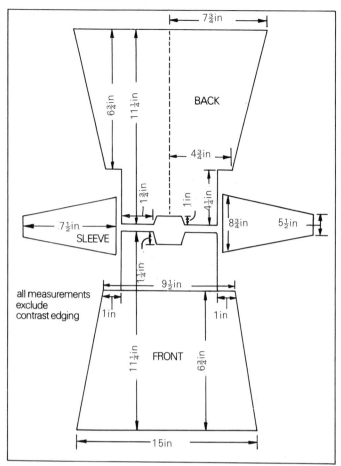

☐ Decrease 1 stitch at the beginning of the next row for the neck edge, then continue in single crochet to the end of the row. Turn.

☐ Continue to decrease 1 stitch at the *beginning* of every other row in the same way until 11 stitches remain. You will be decreasing 1 stitch at the neck edge. Draw yarn through the last loop and fasten off. Return to the stitches at the center of the bodice.

☐ With the right side of the front facing, skip the first 12 stitches for the center neck and rejoin the yarn to the next single crochet.

☐ Complete other side of neck to match the first, decreasing 1 stitch at neck edge on every other row, until 11 stitches remain.

☐ Draw yarn through last loop and fasten off.

To make right back

Using No. 4 steel (1.75mm) hook chain 29. Work the 1st row as given for front. 27 stitches.

☐ Increase 1 stitch at the beginning of the next row as given for front. Increase 1 stitch in the same way at the same edge on every row, keeping the other edge straight for center back opening, until skirt measures the same as the back skirt. There should be 47 stitches. Draw yarn through last loop and fasten off.

To make bodice

Return to chain at beginning of skirt.

☐ With right side of work facing and using a No 0 steel (2.00mm) hook, rejoin yarn to 8th chain from shaped side edge, leaving the first 7 chains for armhole. Work in single crochet to end of row. 22 stitches.

☐ Continue without shaping until bodice measures $3\frac{1}{8}$in (8cm) from beginning, ending at armhole edge.

To shape neck

Work across first 13 single crochets on next row, turn and leave remaining stitches for back neck.

☐ Decrease 1 stitch at beginning of next and then every other row in the same way as for the front until 11 stitches remain and work measures the same as the front to shoulder. Draw yarn through and fasten off.

To make the left back and bodice

Work in the same way as the right back, but work increases at the end of the row instead of at the beginning, on the skirt. Skip 7 chains at the end of the row for the armhole, instead of at the beginning, to reverse the shaping. Work the neck shaping in reverse in exactly the same way.

To make the sleeves

Join shoulder seams using a backstitch seam (see Volume 1, page 29).

☐ Using No. 4 steel (1.75mm) hook and with right side of the front facing, rejoin yarn to inside armhole at shaped side edge. Work 1 row of single crochet up one side of yoke to shoulder, then down other side of yoke to inside edge of armhole. 58 sts. Turn. Work 2 rows in double crochet on these stitches.

☐ Continue working in doubles, decreasing 1 stitch at beginning of every row until sleeve measures $7\frac{1}{2}$in (19cm) from beginning. Draw yarn through last loop and fasten off. Work 2nd sleeve in same way on other side of yoke.

To finish

Darn in all loose ends of yarn on wrong side of smock. Press or block according to directions on the wrapper. With wrong side of work facing join top edges of sleeves to armholes at top of skirt, using a flat seam (see Volume 1, page 29).

☐ Join side and sleeve seams using a backstitch seam.

To work edging

Using main color and No. 4 steel (1.75mm) hook and with right side of left back facing, join yarn to corner and work a row of single crochet all around, up right back, around neck and down left back to corner, working 3 single crochet into each corner stitch and skipping 1 stitch at each corner of inside neck. Draw yarn through last loop and fasten off.

To make contrast edging and ties

With right side of work facing join contrasting color yarn to same corner as before.

☐ Work 1 single crochet all around hem and up back edge to point where skirt is joined to bodice, work 65 chains, then work 1 slip stitch into each chain back to edge again. This forms first tie.

☐ Continue to work in single crochet to first neck edge corner, then work another tie in the same way.

☐ Continue to work in single crochet around neck without skipping 1 stitch at inside neck edges to nect back edge corner. Work another tie in the same way at this corner. Complete the edging working another tie in the same way where yoke joins skirt. Draw yarn through last loop and fasten off. Darn in all ends on wrong side of work.

Baby's sleeveless smock

Size
To fit a baby up to 6 months old.

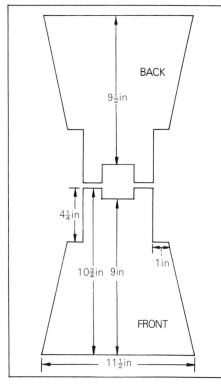

Gauge
24 stitches and 12 rows to 4in (10cm) in doubles using No. 4 steel (1.75mm) hook.

Materials
3oz (50g) of a baby yarn in one color for skirt (A)
3oz (50g) of the same yarn in a contrasting color for the bodice (B)
The striped version also takes 3oz (50g) each of A and B
Nos. 4 and 0 steel (1.75 and 2.00mm) hooks

Note: To make the striped version work two rows in each color down skirt, ending with one row in the first color used. Work the yoke in one color.

To make the front skirt
Using No. 4 steel (1.75mm) hook and A, chain 58.

☐ Work 1 double into 4th chain from hook, 1 double into each chain to end. Turn. 56 doubles. Continue to work in doubles, increasing 1 stitch at the beginning of every row by working 1 stitch into the first stitch after the turning chain, until the skirt measures about 6½in (16.5cm) from the beginning. You should have worked approximately 21 rows and have 76 stitches in all. Draw yarn through last loop and fasten off.

To make the front yoke
Return to the chain at the beginning of the skirt.

☐ With the right side of the skirt facing, using B and No. 0 steel (2.00mm) hook, rejoin yarn to the 8th chain from the side edge, leaving the first 7 chains for the armhole. Work 1 turning chain, then 1 single crochet into each chain, working the last single crochet into the 8th chain from the end, leaving the last 7 chains for the second armhole.

☐ Continue working in rows of single crochet on these stitches for 2⅜in (6cm). Work across first 13 single crochet, turn and work on these stitches only for 1¼in (3cm).

To shape neck
Fasten off. Return to stitches at neck edge. Skip first 18 stitches for center neck. Rejoin yarn to next stitch and complete to

match first side. Draw yarn through and fasten off.

To make the back skirt
Work exactly as given for front skirt.

To make the back yoke
Work exactly as given for front, but work for 3in (7.5cm) before shaping the neck and work for ⅝in (1.5cm) for neck so that the yoke is the same depth as front yoke.

To finish
Darn all loose ends into wrong side of work. Press or block, according to directions on the yarn wrapper. Join side seams using a flat seam.

To work edging and shoulder ties
Using No. 4 steel (1.75mm) hook, B and with right side of front facing, join yarn to underarm at side seam. Work a row of single crochet around armhole to shoulder.

☐ Chain 65 at corner of shoulder, turn and slip stitch into each chain just worked back to shoulder to make the first tie. Work in single crochet to next corner and work another tie in same way. Continue to work around neck in single crochet, skipping 1 stitch at inside neck corners, then work across second shoulder making a tie at each of the corners.

☐ Work down the armhole and around back in same way, making 1 tie at each corner on shoulders. Join last single crochet to first single crochet worked with a slip stitch.

☐ Draw yarn through and fasten off. Darn in any loose ends on wrong side of work using a yarn needle.

*How to shape a double- or triple-crochet fabric
*How to increase and decrease several stitches at each end of a row
*Pattern for an evening sweater

How to shape a double- or triple-crochet fabric

Because of the depth of both the double and triple crochet stitches it is important to shape your work carefully in order to maintain a neat, firm edge on the fabric. Unless a pattern specifically states the method to be used, it is better to work the shaping one stitch in from the edge. This avoids making a step in your fabric, which is particularly noticeable when working long crochet stitches in thicker yarns, and can cause difficulties when finishing the garment.

How to increase a double or triple at each end of a row

Stitches are increased at each end of the row in exactly the same way as for single crochet or half doubles: work two stitches into the stitch after the turning chain at the beginning of the row: then work across the row until only two stitches remain, including the turning chain, then work two stitches into the next stitch; finally, work the last stitch into the turning chain of the previous row.

You will have increased two extra stitches — one stitch at each end of the row within a one-stitch border.

To decrease one double at each end of a row

1 Chain 3 at beginning of row where stitch is to be decreased.

2 Skip the first stitch in the normal way. Wind the yarn around the hook and insert hook into next stitch.

3 Wind yarn around hook and draw through a loop.

4 Wind yarn around hook and draw it through first 2 loops on hook.

5 Wind yarn around hook and insert it into next stitch.

6 Wind yarn around hook and draw a loop through.

7 There are now 4 loops on the hook.

8 Wind yarn around hook and draw it through first 2 loops on hook. 3 loops remain.

9 Wind yarn around hook and draw it through last 3 loops on hook. 2 doubles have been worked together to decrease 1 stitch.

10 Work 1 double into each double until 3 stitches remain unworked. Do not forget to count the turning chain as 1 stitch.

11 Work the next 2 doubles together in the same way as at beginning of row. 1 stitch decreased at end of row.

12 Work the last double into the turning chain of previous row.

To decrease one triple at each end of a row

1 Chain 4 at beginning of row where stitch is to be decreased.

2 Skip the first stitch in the normal way. Wind the yarn twice around the hook and insert the hook into the next stitch.

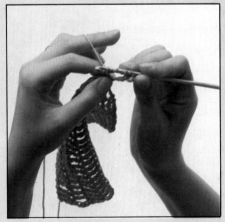

3 Wind yarn around hook and draw through a loop. 4 loops on the hook.

continued

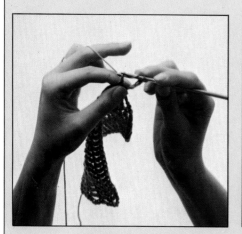

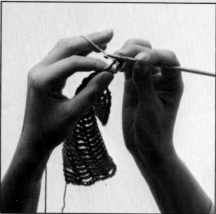

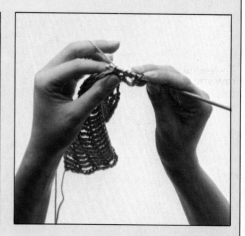

4 Wind yarn around hook and draw it through first 2 loops on hook.

5 Wind yarn around hook and draw it through next 2 loops on hook. 2 loops remain.

6 Wind yarn twice around hook and insert hook into next stitch.

7 Wind yarn around hook and draw a loop through. 5 loops on the hook.

8 Repeat steps 4 and 5. 3 loops remain on hook.

9 Wind yarn around hook and draw it through all 3 loops on hook. 2 triples have been worked together to decrease 1 stitch.

10 Work 1 triple into each stitch across row until 3 stitches remain unworked. Do not forget to count the turning chain as 1 stitch.

11 Work the next 2 triples together in the same way as at beginning of row. 1 stitch decreased.

12 Work the last triple into the turning chain at the end of the row.

How to increase or decrease several stitches at each end of a row

It is possible to increase several stitches at each end of a row by working extra chains for each additional stitch required. When increasing stitches at the beginning of the row you will also need to add extra chains to allow for the turning chain, remembering that the number of turning chains will vary according to the kind of stitch being worked. For example, if you are going to add an extra four single crochets you will need to make five chains in all. For four doubles you will need to make six chains in all. The method for decreasing several stitches at the beginning or end of a row is the same for all crochet stitches. Work in slip stitch over the number of stitches to be decreased at the beginning of the row, then work a slip stitch into the next stitch and make the correct number of turning chains before working across the row in the normal way. To decrease several stitches at the end of the row simply leave the required number of stitches unworked, remembering always to count the turning chain as one stitch, then turn and work back along the next row. Since the technique used for increasing several stitches at each end of the row is the same for all stitches, follow the working method given for single crochet but substitute the correct number of turning chains for the stitch being used.

To increase several single crochets at each end of a row

1 Work the extra number of chains you need at the beginning of the row, e.g. 5 chains for 4 single crochets.

2 Work the first single crochet into the 3rd chain from the hook, then 1 single crochet into each extra chain.

3 Continue to work in single crochet across row until 2 stitches remain. This will include the turning chain.

4 Leave the working loop on an extra hook.

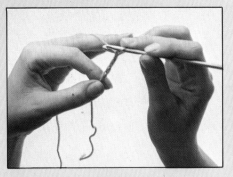

5 With an extra piece of the correct yarn chain the exact number of extra stitches you need; e.g. 4 chains for 4 single crochets.

6 Join this length of chains to the end of the row with a slip stitch. Fasten off yarn.

7 Return to the working loop and work 1 single crochet into each of the last 2 stitches.

8 Work 1 single crochet into each of the extra chains, 4 single crochets increased at each end of row.

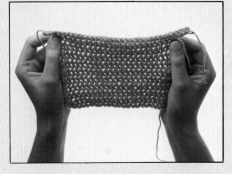

9 Work in single crochet across all stitches on the next row, including those just made.

Fluffy and flattering

Make something special for winter evenings. This glamorous mohair-look sweater, with batwing sleeves and bloused shape, has ribbons threaded through for added fashion interest.

Size
To fit 32½ to 38in (83–97cm) bust. Length to shoulder, 24in (61cm). Sleeve seam, 2½in (6.5cm).

Gauge
9 stitches and 4 rows to 4in (10cm) worked in triples on a size I (6mm) hook.

Materials
Total of 12oz (325g) of a mohair-type yarn
Size G (4.5mm) crochet hook
Size I (6mm) crochet hook
10yd (9m) of 1in (2.5cm)-wide ribbon

Back and front (made in one piece)
☐ Begin at lower edge of front. Using size I (6mm) hook, chain 42 loosely.
Shape front
☐ Work 1 triple into 5th chain from hook, 1 triple into same chain to increase 1 stitch, 1 triple into each chain until 2 chains remain unworked, work 2 triples into next chain to increase 1 stitch, 1 triple into last chain. Turn. 41 triples.
☐ Work 4 chains to count as first triple, skip first triple, 2 triples into next triple to increase 1 stitch, 1 triple into each stitch until 2 triples remain unworked, work 2 triples into next stitch

to increase 1 stitch, work last triple into turning chain of previous row. Turn.
☐ Repeat the last row 14 times more. There will now be 71 triples.
Work sleeves
☐ Place a marker at each end of last row to show beginning of sleeves.
☐ Work 5 rows triples without shaping.
Make neck opening
☐ Work over first 26 triples, work 19 chains loosely, then skip next 19 triples for neck opening, work 1 triple into each stitch to end of row. Turn. Work over first 26 triples, work 1 triple into each of next 19 chains, work 1 triple into each stitch to end of row. Turn. 71 triples.
☐ Work 4 rows without shaping. Place a marker at each end of last row to show end of sleeves.
Shape back
☐ Chain 4 to count as first stitch, work next 2 triples together to decrease 1 stitch, work 1 triple into each stitch until 3 stitches remain unworked, work next 2 triples together to decrease 1 stitch, work last triple into turning chain of previous row. Turn.
☐ Repeat last row 15 times more. 39 triples remain.
☐ Draw yarn through and fasten off.

To make back waistband
☐ Using size G (4.5mm) hook chain 12. Work 1 double into 4th chain from hook, then 1 double into each chain to end. Turn. 10 doubles.
☐ Chain 3 to count as first double, work 1 double into back loop only of each stitch to end. Turn.
☐ Repeat last row until waistband is long enough to fit along lower edge.
☐ Draw yarn through and fasten off.

To make front waistband
Work exactly as given for back waistband.

To make cuffs
☐ Work as given for waistband until cuff fits along sleeve edge between markers.
☐ Work another cuff in the same way.

To finish
☐ Darn in all loose ends on wrong side using a blunt-ended yarn needle.
☐ Thread ribbon through (over and under every 3 stitches, every 3rd row); secure the ends.
☐ Using a flat seam sew waistbands to lower edge of back and front.
☐ Using a flat seam sew cuffs to sleeves between markers.
☐ Join underarm and side seams.

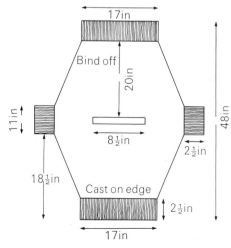

Crochet / COURSE 8

*Working horizontal stripes
*Working vertical stripes —
 two methods
*Working diagonal stripes
*Start using abbreviations
*Pattern for a striped rug

Working horizontal stripes

Stripes are a good way to add extra color or detail to a garment. They can be in sharp, contrasting colors or subtle shades. They can cross the fabric horizontally, vertically or diagonally. By varying the width of each stripe you can achieve a pleasant random effect.

Horizontal stripes are easy to work, especially if you use an even number of rows in each color so that each color begins and ends at the same edge. Our sample uses two colors, called A and B, and is worked in single crochet.

1 Make the desired number of chains with A. Work two rows with A, but do not complete the last stitch of the second row; leave two loops on hook.

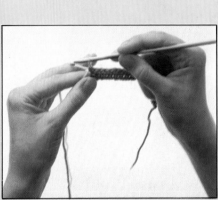

2 Loop B over hook and draw it through working loop. This completes the last stitch. Do not break off A.

3 Turn the work. Twist B over and under A to hold A in place. Each color is carried up the side of the work until it is needed again.

4 Work the next two rows in B. Do not complete the last stitch; leave two loops on the hook.

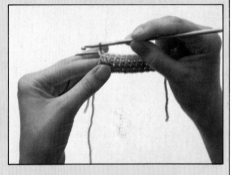

5 Pick up A and complete stitch in A.

6 Turn the work. Twist A over and under B to hold B in place.

7 Continue to work stripes in A and B, carrying yarns up the side until the desired number of stripes has been worked. Fasten off.

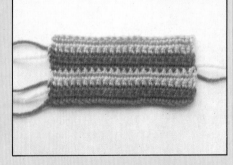

8 If you work an uneven number of rows in any color you will need to cut off the yarn and rejoin it at the other edge as shown.

Paul Williams

15

Working vertical stripes
The carrying method

This simple method is used when the stripes are only two or three stitches wide and the yarn is not too thick. The yarn is carried across the back of the work. Our sample is made in single crochet and uses two colors, A and B.

1 Chain 19 with A; with A work one single crochet.

2 Change from A to B on next stitch by completing stitch with B. The first three stitches (turning chain counts as first stitch) will be in A.

3 Wind B around A. Keep A at back of work.

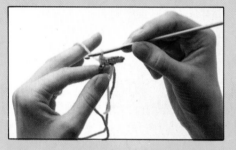

4 Work next two stitches in B.

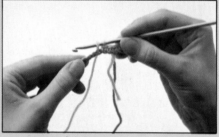

5 Insert hook into next stitch and draw through a loop. Leave B at back of work.

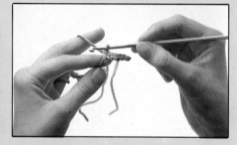

6 Pick up A. Carry A over B and complete stitch in A, being careful not to pull the carried yarn too tight. There will be three stitches in B.

7 Continue to work three stitches in A and three in B across row in same way, but complete last stitch in B.

8 Turn and work first two stitches in B, insert hook into next stitch and draw through a loop. A will be at front of work.

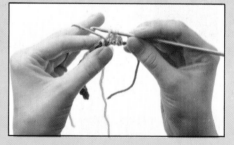

9 Bring B to front of work, then take A over B to back of work.

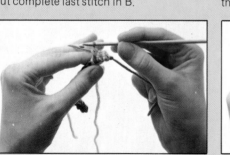

10 Complete stitch with A.

11 Continue to work in stripes across row, changing colors in same way each time, but complete last stitch in A.

12 Repeat these two rows until stripe pattern is complete. Fasten off.

Paul Williams

The weaving method

The weaving method is used when the stripes are more than three stitches wide. The yarn being carried across the back of the work is linked to the top of one of the stitches in the stripe. The yarn is woven neatly into the back of the fabric.

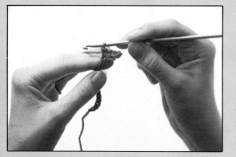

1 Chain 21 in A, and work first three single crochets in A.

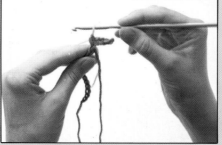

2 Change from A to B on next stitch by completing stitch with B. The first five stitches (including turning chain) will be in A.

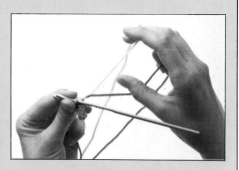

3 Wind B around A. Keep A at back of work.

4 Work next two stitches in B. As you work the third stitch in B, hold A against the top edge of the row and crochet over it with the next stitch, taking care not to pull the carried yarn too tight.

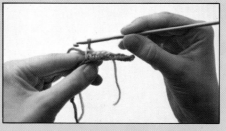

5 Keeping A at the back, work two more stitches in B, changing to A on the second stitch. Five stitches have now been worked in A and five in B.

6 Continue to work five stitches in A and five in B across the row in the same way, linking the color being woven to the third stitch of every stripe, but complete the last stitch in B.

7 Turn and work the first four stitches in B, remembering to count the turning chain as the first stitch, and noting that A will be at front of work.

8 Insert hook into next stitch and draw through a loop.

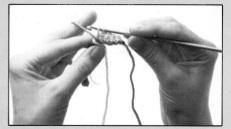

9 Bring B to front of work, then take A to back of work.

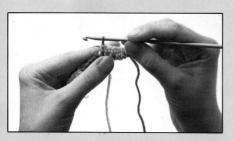

10 Complete stitch with A.

11 Continue to work in stripes across row, changing and linking colors in the same way each time, but complete last stitch in A.

12 Repeat these two rows until stripe pattern is complete. Fasten off.

Paul Williams

17

Working diagonal stripes

These are worked in exactly the same way as vertical stripes, except that one stitch on each stripe is moved either to the right or to the left on every row to slant the stripes diagonally from right to left or left to right.

Carry the yarn across the back of the work and change the colors as needed in the same way as when working vertical stripes.

Paul Williams

Start using abbreviations

Crochet has its own technical terms and a special language—a kind of shorthand—for describing directions in a clear, concise way. Without this shorthand, the directions for any but the simplest crochet would be far too long and tedious to follow.

The abbreviations given here are for simple techniques that you already know: gradually these and other crochet abbreviations will be introduced into patterns in the courses. As you gain more practice in crochet, you will find following the abbreviations becomes easy and almost automatic.

ch	=	chain
sc	=	single crochet
dc	=	double crochet
hdc	=	half double crochet
tr	=	triple crochet
dtr	=	double triple
st(s)	=	stitch(es)

Striped rug

This colorful rug will bring warmth to any fireside and last for many years. It can be made by using up leftover yarns, and is finished with a crab stitch edging.

Gauge
8½ sts and 10 rows to 4in (10cm) over sc.

Size
18×36in (45×90cm)

Materials
6oz (150g) rug yarn in each of the following: yellow (A), gold (B), red-orange (C), cherry red (D), fuchsia (E), green (J)
4oz (50g) rug yarn in each of the following: purple (F), blue (G), blue-green (H)
Size K (7.00mm) crochet hook

To make
Using A and size K (7.00mm) hook, make 39ch, 1sc into 2nd ch from hook, 1sc into each ch to end, turn.
Next row 1ch, 1sc into each sc to end, turn.
Rep this row throughout, cutting and leaving the end after each color, working in a sequence of 6 rows A, 6 rows B, 6 rows C, 6 rows D, 6 rows E, 4 rows F, 4 rows G, 4 rows H, 6 rows J. Now work in reverse order beginning with 4 rows H, then 4 rows G, finishing with 6 rows A. Fasten off and darn in all ends.

Edging
Using J, join yarn approx ⅜in (1cm) inside from a corner and work in crab stitch edging (sc from left to right). Work 3 sts into each corner, around complete edge of rug, finishing with a sl st into same place as join.

Technique tip

Changing colored yarns

A new colored yarn should be introduced at the end of each row for a regular striped effect. The loose ends are then darned in neatly on the wrong side of the work, running the yarn through several stitches of the same color before trimming the ends. This makes the back of work neat.

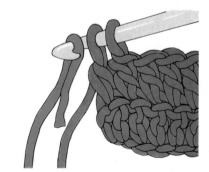

Introduce a new yarn on the triple (shown here) and double triple stitches by working the new yarn at the final stage when two loops remain on the hook. Continue working across the row in the normal way.

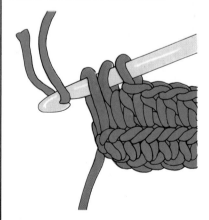

To join a new color at the end of the row for half double crochet stitch, introduce the yarn when three loops remain on the hook. Leave a loose end that is long enough to be darned in at a later stage. Pull the old yarn gently at the side of the work to tighten the join.

When changing color in the center of the row for staggered stripes or picture patterns, join in the new yarn at the last stage of the previous stitch. Keep the yarn at the back of the work when completing the row.

Lindsay Blow

*Working with separate balls of yarn
*Working longer stitches
*Pattern for a shawl

A tremendous variety of shapes and patterns can be achieved in crochet by using different colors. The possibilities include motifs repeated at regular intervals across your fabric, large motifs such as diamonds or rectangles, blocks of colors worked in a random pattern and a variety of colors for a patchwork effect.

Working with separate balls of yarn

When the motif being worked is small and is repeated several times at regular intervals across the fabric, the yarn can be carried across the back of the work in the same way as for vertical stripes. Large motifs or patchwork patterns, however, should be worked using separate balls of yarn for each color. This avoids wasting yarn.

The separate balls can be wound on a shaped piece of cardboard which acts like a bobbin and helps to prevent the different colors from becoming tangled. Our sample shows the technique used in wide stripes of single crochet and uses two colors, called A and B.

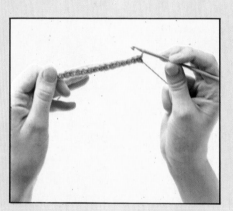

1 Make 31 chains with A and work 30 single crochets into chain. Turn.

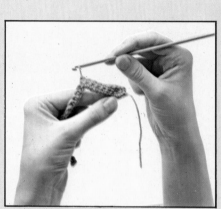

2 Work the first 9 single-crochet stitches with A.

3 Insert hook into next stitch and draw a loop through.

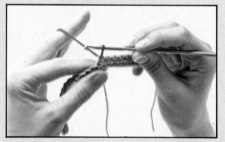

4 Draw next color through working loop to complete stitch.

5 Wind B around A at back of work, passing B under and then over A. This winding of one yarn around the other prevents a gap where the stripes or shapes meet.

6 Work next 9 single crochets in B, then change from B to second ball of A repeating steps 3 and 4.

7 Repeat step 5 winding A around B.

8 Work the last 10 single crochets in A.

Paul Williams

9 Turn and work first 9 stitches in A. The wrong side of the work will be facing.

10 Insert hook into next stitch and draw a loop through.

11 Bring A to front of work, take B to back of work and complete stitch with B.

12 Continue to change colors at beginning of each stripe across the row in the same way, keeping the yarn not in use at the back of the work each time.

13 Work at least 10 rows in this way so that you are familiar with the working method and can cope with both colors easily.

14 Sample showing the wrong side of the fabric.

Working longer stitches

Single crochet is really the ideal stitch for working motifs into a fabric. Because it is a shallow stitch, you can easily achieve a sloping edge on a motif; with deeper stitches, changes in color made on a diagonal will produce a stepped effect. In working rectangles or squares, however, you can use double crochet or even deeper stitches effectively.

1 When working longer stitches such as triple crochet, make 31 chains, then work 28 triples.

2 On the second row, work across the first 13 triples (14 triples including turning chain).

3 Insert hook into next stitch and work chains with next color, to stand as next stitch (i.e. 4 for triple crochet).

4 You will now have 2 loops on the hook, one in each of the two colors.

5 Draw loop at top of chain through loop of first color. Continue to the end of the row.

Paul Williams

Soft, muted shawl

Make this beautiful, soft shawl in muted shades as big as you fancy. Just work from the point up and finish when you like.

Gary Warren

Size
Length at center, $36\frac{1}{4}$in (92cm).

Materials
16oz (400g) of a medium-weight mohair-type yarn
This shawl took 6oz (150g) each in gray-green and pink; 4oz (100g) in cream
Size H (5.00mm) crochet hook

Gauge
11 triples and $4\frac{1}{4}$ rows to 4in (10cm).

To make shawl

Using green, make 5ch.
Base row Work 2tr into 5ch from hook. Turn.
Next row 4ch to count as first tr, work 1tr into first tr — so increasing 1tr, 1tr into next tr, 2tr into the turning ch of previous row. Turn. 5tr.
Next row 4ch 2tr into first tr, 2tr into each tr to end. Turn. 9tr.
Next row 4ch. 1tr into first tr, 2tr into next tr, work 1tr into each tr to within last 2tr, work 2tr into each of last 2tr — so increasing 2tr at each end of the row. Turn.
Repeat the last row twice more, but join in pink on last tr. 21tr. Cut off green.
Continuing to increase 2tr at each end of every row, work in color sections as follows:
Next row Work over first 9tr, joining cream on the 9th of these tr (so having 11tr worked in pink), with cream work to end of row.
Work 3 more rows using pink and cream. Cut off yarns.
Work 4 rows using green and pink. Cut off yarns.
Work 4 rows using cream and green. Cut off yarns.
Work 4 rows using pink and cream. Cut off yarns.
Work 4 rows using green and pink. Cut off yarns.
Repeat the last 12 rows once more. Fasten off.

Working geometric patterns from a chart

More complicated patterns are sometimes worked from a chart, which shows the motif or pattern on graph paper. This method of representing the motif eliminates the need for lengthy row-by-row directions. The charts are clear and easy to follow, so do not be put off by their seeming complexity.

Each square on the graph represents one stitch, and each horizontal line represents one row. The motif as represented on the graph will not be in proportion, since a square will not be the same width or depth as a stitch; the chart should be used as a plan only.

Begin reading the chart from the bottom right-hand corner, so that the first row is read from right to left. This will be the right side of the work; the second row, which is worked on the wrong side, will be read from left to right.

Where a motif is to be repeated a number of times during the course of a row, the chart will show only one complete pattern repeat, plus the stitches to be worked at

each end of the row. The stitches within the pattern repeat should be repeated as many times as stated in the directions, followed by the stitches to be worked at the end of the row. These end stitches will be the first stitches of the following row.

Our sample is worked in two colors, coded A and B, in single crochet. A is represented by an X on the chart and B by a blank square. Carry the yarn not in use across the back of the work.

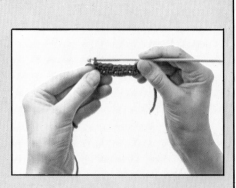

1 Make 11 chains with A; begin at bottom right-hand corner of chart and work 2 rows in A. These will be rows 1 and 2 on the chart.

2 Join B ready for next row.

3 With right side of the work facing, work row 3 of chart from right to left.

A = ✖ MAROON
B = ☐ CAMEL

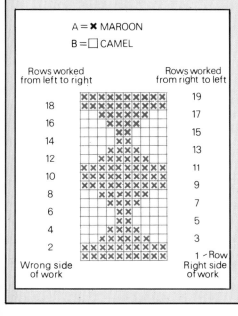

Rows worked from left to right		Rows worked from right to left
18		19
16		17
14		15
12		13
10		11
8		9
6		7
4		5
2		3
Wrong side of work		1 - Row Right side of work

4 Turn. With wrong side of the work facing, work row 4 of chart from left to right.

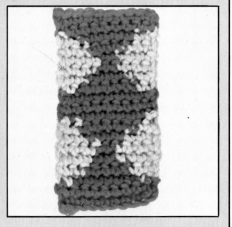

5 Continue to work each row in same way until motif is complete.

Homespun vest

Try out your own color combinations and make this delightful patchwork-look vest. A rich blend of colors gives it a really warm, homespun look.

Gary Warren

Sizes
To fit 32/34in (83/87cm) bust.
Length at center back, 18in (46cm).

Materials
Total of 9oz (250g) of knitting worsted
This garment took 3oz (75g) of knitting worsted in copper and rust and 1oz (25g) in camel; also 4oz (100g) in brown tweed
Size E (3.50mm) crochet hook
Five buttons

Gauge
17 doubles and 9 rows to 4in (10cm).

Back

Using rust, make 61ch.
Base row 1dc into 4th ch from hook, 1dc into each ch to end. Turn 59dc.
Working in dc throughout proceed as follows:
Beginning with row 2 on chart, work patchwork design until row 11 has been worked. Work 2dc into first and last dc on next row — so increasing 1dc at each end of the row. Increase 1dc at each end of every other row 4 more times. 69dc. Fasten off.
Shape armholes
Next row Join tweed to 6th dc from side edge and work 3ch to count as first dc, work to within last 5dc. Turn. 59dc.
Continuing to follow the chart, work the first 2dc and the last 2dc together on the next row — so decreasing 1dc at each end of the row. Decrease 1dc at each end of next 7 rows. 43dc. Work 9 rows straight.
Fasten off.

Right front

Using rust, make 4ch.
Base row Work 2dc into 4th ch from hook. Turn. 3dc.
Beginning with row 2 on chart, work patchwork design shaping as follows:
Increase 2dc at each end of next 3 rows. 15dc. Now increase 2dc at end of next row and at this same edge on following row. 19dc.
Next row Work to end increasing 2dc at end of row; do not turn work but make 11ch for side edge extension. Turn.
Next row 1dc into 4th ch from hook, 1dc into each ch and dc to end. Turn. 30dc.
Work straight until row 18 has been worked.
Increase 1dc at end of next row and

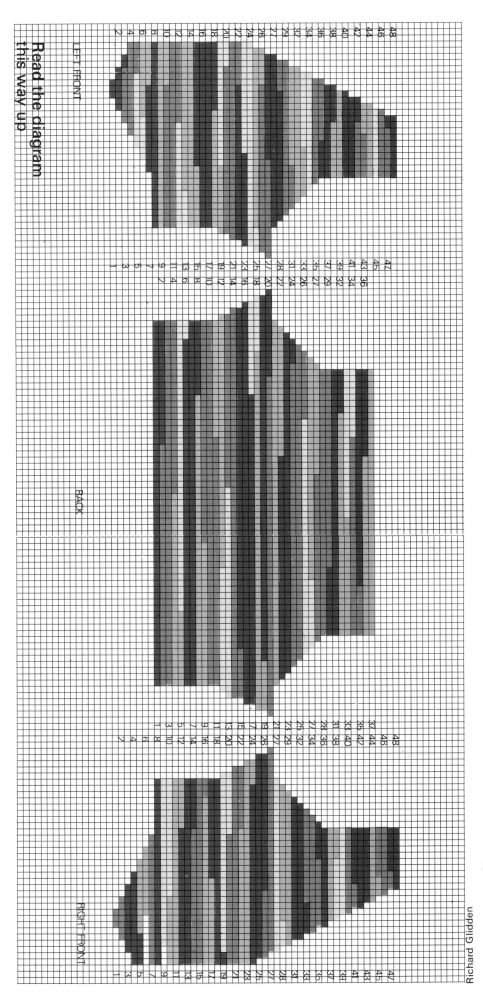

Read the diagram this way up

LEFT FRONT

BACK

RIGHT FRONT

Richard Glidden

every other row 2 more times. Work 1 row straight.

Shape front edge
Continuing to increase 1dc at side edge, decrease 1dc at the beginning of the next and third row. 33dc. Fasten off.

Shape armhole
Next row Join camel to 6th dc from side edge; work 3ch to count as first dc, work to end. Turn.
Continuing to shape front edge on every other row, decrease 1dc at armhole edge on next 8 rows. 16dc. Keeping armhole edge straight continue to shape front edge until 10dc remain. Work 1 row. Fasten off.

Left front
Work as given for right front, reversing shaping and working side edge extension as follows: At end of row 7 make 9ch using a separate ball of rust; fasten off and lay aside. Work row 8 to end of row, then work across the 9ch, making 30dc.

The border
Join shoulder and side seams using a flat seam. With right side facing, join tweed and work a row of sc evenly all around outer edge, working 2sc into each st at front points and finishing by working a slip stitch into the first sc. Continuing to work 2sc into 2sc at points, work one round in rust, then one round in cream, making 5 evenly spaced buttonholes on the right front by working 2ch and skipping 2sc. Next, work one round in brick working 2sc into each buttonhole, and one round in tweed. Fasten off.

Armhole borders
Following the color sequence as given for the border, work 5 rows of sc evenly all around armhole.

To finish
Block according to yarn used. Sew on the buttons.

What is "gauge"?

Gauge is one of the most important elements in successful knitting, yet it is often overlooked. It involves the relationship of yarn to needle size and the way you control the yarn. Knitting should be an enjoyable pastime, not a chore; relax and allow the yarn to run easily over your fingers — they have a function similar to the tension control of a sewing machine. As you practice with different types of yarn, you will notice that thicker yarns require looser control while thinner yarns need a tighter one: any variation in control within a piece of knitting gives it an irregular appearance.

Remember that the tightness of your work is personal to you, since two people rarely work the same way; this is why it is unwise to let another person complete a piece of knitting you have started. To see— and feel what gauge is about—try the following experiment with a ball of yarn and a range of needle sizes:

You need a ball of knitting worsted and a selection of knitting needles, preferably a complete set ranging from No. 00 to 11 (2-7½mm). Using No. 11 (7½mm) needles cast on 24 stitches and work six rows in stockinette stitch. (To prevent the fabric from curling, purl the second and next to last stitches on every knit row.)

Change the needles one size smaller. Mark the change by working one purl row to make a ridge across the right side. Work five rows in stockinette stitch. Continue in this way until you have worked through the whole range of needles.

The tapering look of the finished sample indicates that you can shape a piece of knitting without complicated increasing and decreasing, but simply by changing the needle size. The pattern for the baggy sweater on page 28 puts this method into practical use.

Nos. 00, 0, 1 and 2 (2–3mm) needles
The smallest needle sizes give a hard, stiff fabric with tiny crowded stitches.

Nos. 3, 4, 5 and 6 ($3\frac{1}{4}$–$4\frac{1}{2}$mm) needles
This range of needle sizes works perfectly in conjunction with knitting worsted, to produce neat, firm stitches in a soft elastic fabric.

Nos. 7, 8 and 9 (5–6mm) needles
These sizes are too large for this knitting worsted. It is hard to keep the stitches neat and the quality of the pattern is lost.

Nos. 10, $10\frac{1}{2}$ and 11 ($6\frac{1}{2}$–$7\frac{1}{2}$mm) needles
These needles are extra large for the yarn: they produce a soft fabric unsuitable for most garments as it has difficulty in retaining the shape. Using a softer yarn, such as mohair, results in a warm fabric with an almost cellular quality.

Getting the correct gauge for a pattern

Most patterns give a gauge guide that states the number of stitches and rows to a measurement using the recommended yarn and needles. This is the designer's gauge and all measurements in the knitting pattern are based on it.

If you want to end up with a garment that fits, you must achieve the same gauge as the designer. Even one stitch too many or too few in every 4in (10cm) makes a significant difference in the size of a piece of knitting, especially with a thick yarn. If ten stitches should measure 4in (10cm) and you knit only nine stitches in every 4in (10cm) the front of a sweater that should measure $19\frac{3}{4}$in (50cm) across is going to be 2in (5cm) too big. The back of the sweater will be the same, and the finished garment will be 4in (10cm) bigger than it should.

Make a swatch to check your gauge before you start work. Knitting course 2 tells how to check simple gauge; both stitch and row gauge must be correct in complicated patterns.

An accurate stitch gauge is necessary in most patterns to obtain the correct width; in some instances the row gauge is important too. For instance, row gauge must be correct when you are increasing or decreasing over a specific measurement to shape a garment or when you are working a garment from side edge to side edge so that the number of rows, not stitches, determines the width.

If you obtain the correct stitch gauge, but the number of rows is slightly more or less than stated, ignore the difference and continue to work—unless the circumstances are special, as described above. Only make more swatches if the row gauge is drastically wrong; in this case it is fairly certain that the stitch gauge is also wrong.

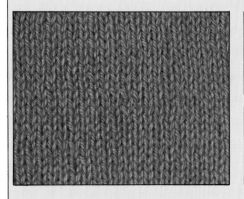

1 Patterns often quote the gauge over a stockinette stitch fabric, e.g. 21 sts and 27 rows to 4in (10cm) in stockinette st. Make a 5in (12cm) stockinette stitch sample using a few more stitches than stated in the gauge guide.

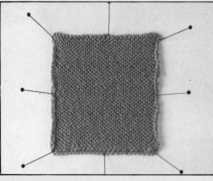

2 Pin the sample down, without stretching it, on a flat surface such as an ironing board. The stitches and rows are more distinctive on the reverse side of stockinette stitch.

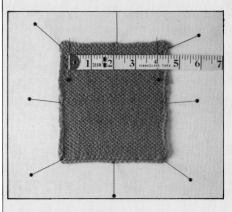

3 Count 21 stitches on your sample and mark with pins. Check their measurement with a tape measure. If there are less than 21 to 4in (10cm), use a smaller needle, if there are more than 21, use a larger one.

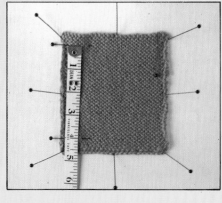

4 Each horizontal ridge represents a row of stockinette stitch. Insert 1 pin between ridges and count 27 rows, inserting the second pin in the hollow after the last ridge counted. Use a tape measure to check the measurement of these rows.

continued

Paul Williams

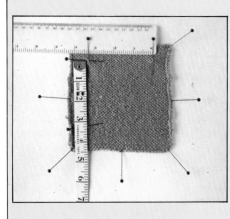

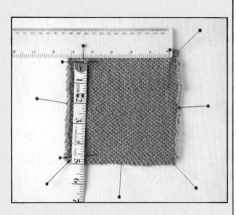

5 This sample it too tight; 27 rows make less than 4in (10cm): the stitch gauge is also incorrect. Make another sample with needles one size larger: try progressively larger needles until the gauge is absolutely correct.

6 Here the knitting is too loose; the 27 rows measure more than 4in (10cm): again the stitch gauge is wrong. Use smaller needles to make another sample. It doesn't matter how many times you change the needle size as long as you end up with the correct gauge.

Big, baggy sweater

This loose, cuddly sweater is shaped simply by changing the size of your needles. Back and front are exactly the same and it can be made up in no time.

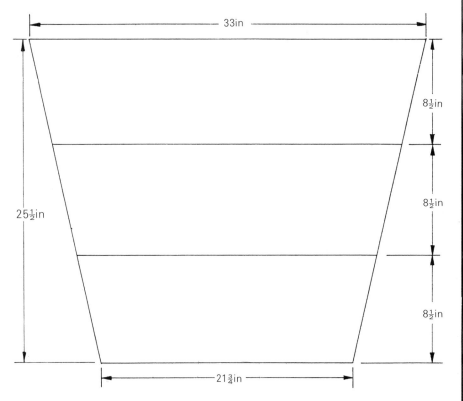

Measurements
These directions are for the measurements shown on the diagram. The top is very loose and fits a range of bust sizes from 32½ to 36in (83 to 92cm). If you want to make the top larger or smaller, cast on about two stiches more or less for each ⅜in (1cm) difference. Knit the top to any

length you like. Remember you need more or less yarn according to the size you make: in general allow approximately 1oz (25g) for each 2in (5cm) you add to the bust size.

Materials
Total of 8oz (200g) of fine mohair-type yarn
1 pair each Nos. 4, 8, and 11 (3¾, 5½ and 7½mm) knitting needles

Gauge
18 sts and 40 rows to 4in (10cm) in garter st on No. 4 (3¾mm) needles.

Front
Using No. 4 (3¾mm) needles cast on 98 sts for lower edge. Always slipping first st of every row, work 8½in (22cm) in garter st.
☐ Change to No. 8 (5½mm) needles. Work another 8½in (22cm) in garter st.
☐ Change to No. 11 (7½mm) needles. Continue in garter st until work measures 25½in (66cm) from cast-on edge.
Bind off very loosely: if possible, use one size larger needle.

Back
Make the back the same as the front.

To finish
Do not press at any stage.

☐ Using a backstitch, join shoulder seams for approximately 11in (28cm) from each armhole edge. Using a flat seam, join side seams leaving 8¾in (22cm) open for armholes.

Learn your abbreviations

Knitting has its own technical terms and a special language—a kind of shorthand—for describing directions in a clear, concise way. Without this shorthand, the directions for any but the simplest knitting are far too long and tedious to follow.

The abbreviations here are for simple techniques you already know: gradually these and other general knitting notation will be introduced into patterns in Stitch by Stitch. As you become more proficient in your knitting, you will find that following the abbreviations becomes very easy and automatic.

K = knit
P = purl
st(s) = stitch(es)
K1, p1 rib = knit 1, purl 1 (single) rib

Every knitter knows the frustration of not being able to obtain the yarn recommended in a pattern. Substitution is usually possible if you are aware of the pitfalls. Once you understand the basic principles of gauge and how they apply in patterns, you can guard against the wrong choice of yarn.

Always choose another yarn in the same category as the original, i.e. sport, bulky,

mohair: sales clerks in knitting stores are often an excellent source of advice on yarns.

It is essential to check the gauge with the recommended needles. The thickness of yarns is not standardized; even widely available knitting worsted varies in thickness from brand to brand. When you are substituting a yarn, buy one ball to see if it will work with your pattern before you buy the complete amount.

Note: At this stage do not try to substitute a different stitch from the one used in the pattern. Even when the same yarn and needles are used, different stitch patterns create their own, widely varying gauges, and the number of stitches throughout the pattern may have to be altered. This is too complicated for a relatively inexperienced knitter, but a later chapter will show you how to do it.

Substituting yarns

1 This sample shows the correct gauge for a sweater that you want to knit using knitting worsted, No. 5 (4mm) needles and the seed stitch pattern recommended in the pattern. Here there are 20 stitches and 37 rows to 4in (10cm), as quoted in the pattern; all the designer's calculations are based on this gauge.

2 You want to make the sweater in a bouclé yarn that appears roughly similar in thickness to knitting worsted.

3 Make a gauge swatch in seed stitch with the bouclé yarn and the needles recommended in the pattern.

4 The yarn is so textured it is difficult to count the stitches and rows in this sample, but it contains the same number as the knitting worsted swatch, so the gauge is clearly different. Also, the effectiveness of the stitch pattern is lost in the texture of the yarn, making the yarn unsuitable.

5 Next, you decide to try substituting some Shetland-type yarn. Make another sample using the recommended needles. The gauge here is 19 stitches and 35 rows to 4in (10cm); this is too loose, and your sweater will be slightly too large. Knit another sample using smaller needles.

6 Try one size smaller. This time there are 20 stitches and 37 rows to 4in (10cm) — the same as in the original knitting worsted. The seed stitch looks as attractive in this Shetland-type yarn as it does in the original yarn.

Shoestring

Big yellow shoebag

Cleverly made from a large yellow dust cloth, this shoebag would certainly be easy for your child to identify among the others at school.

Materials
> Yellow dust cloth (or piece of yellow flannel) measuring $19 \times 23\frac{1}{2}$in (48×60cm)
> 1yd (1m) red cord
> 1 skein stranded embroidery floss in bright red
> Red sewing thread
> Graph paper
> Tracing paper
> Dressmaker's carbon paper

1 Fold the shorter edges of the dust cloth to meet at the center, overlapping $\frac{1}{4}$in (6mm) and making both sides of the bag equal widths. Pin in place. Write the words "left" and "right" on graph paper, making them twice the size they are here. Trace the words and carefully transfer them to the appropriate side of the folded dust cloth using dressmaker's carbon paper. Center the words on each side, 5in (13cm) from the bottom edge.
2 Unpin the dust cloth and embroider both words in heavy chain stitch using three strands of the embroidery floss.
3 Turn over and baste a double hem $1\frac{3}{4}$in (4.5cm) wide on the right side at the top edge of the dust cloth. Stitch close to both folds of the hem to form a casing.
4 Refold the dust cloth as before and pin in place. Leaving the casing open, stitch two parallel lines down the center front close to the edge of the dust cloth, through the three layers of fabric. This divides the bag into two compartments, one for each shoe. Stitch twice along the bottom, close to the edge.
5 Thread the cord through the casing at the top of the bag and knot the ends.

S. Wells

John Hutchinson

each square = ½ in

Knitting / COURSE 9

Simple increasing on knit and purl rows

At some point in your knitting you will need to shape the fabric to make it wider by increasing the number of stitches in the row.

There are various ways of making extra stitches, depending on how you want the finished increase to look. Making two stitches out of one is the simplest, most popular method and can be worked anywhere in the row. It is a convenient way to shape side edges, either increasing into the first or last stitches in a row, or increasing one stitch from the end, to maintain a slightly neater edge.

The abbreviation for this technique is "inc one st". If a pattern says "increase a stitch" then you should use this method; if another technique for increasing is specified you must follow the precise instructions that are given in the pattern.

To make two stitches out of one on a knit row

1 Insert right-hand (RH) needle from front to back into first stitch in a knit row.

2 Wind yarn under and over RH needle in a clockwise direction.

3 Draw a new stitch through the loop on the left-hand (LH) needle in the same way as knitting.

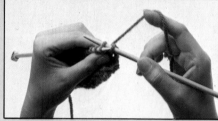

4 Twist RH needle point in a clockwise direction until it lies behind LH needle point: there is a new loop on the RH needle and the stitch you are working into remains on the LH needle.

5 Insert RH needle from right to left into back of stitch on LH needle.

6 Wind yarn under and over RH needle in a clockwise direction.

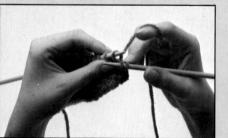

7 Draw a new stitch through the loop on the LH needle in the same way as knitting.

8 Slip the first stitch off the LH needle in the usual way.

9 There are now two stitches on the RH needle made by increasing in the first stitch of the row.

Paul Williams

32

To make two stitches out of one on a purl row

1 Insert RH needle from back to front into front of the first stitch in a purl row.

2 Wind yarn over top and around RH needle in a counterclockwise direction.

3 Use LH thumb to gently push RH needle point back through loop on LH needle.

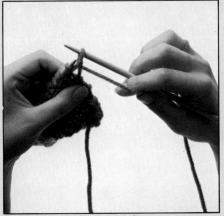

4 There is a new loop on the RH needle, and the stitch you are working into remains on the LH needle.

5 Insert RH needle from left to right into back of stitch on LH needle: hold top of loop clear with left thumbnail until needle is well inserted between front and back strands.

6 Wind yarn over top and around RH needle in a counterclockwise direction.

7 Use LH thumb to gently push RH needle point back through loop on LH needle.
8 Twist RH needle upward and forward.

9 Slip the first stitch off the LH needle in the usual way.

10 There are now two stitches on the RH needle made by increasing in the first stitch in the row.

Paul Williams

Simple decreasing on knit and purl rows

The usual way to decrease a stitch is to knit or purl two stitches together, combining them to form a single stitch. This technique is abbreviated as "K2 tog" on a knit row or "P2 tog" on a purl row. You can use this method at any point in a row, as well as for shaping side edges. The steepness of shaped edges, such as a raglan armhole or the triangular form-ation of the squares in the jacket pattern given at the end of this chapter, depends on the frequency of decreasing. Working stitches together at the beginning and end of every fourth or more rows gives a gradually tapering edge, while decreasing on every row or every other row gives a sharper incline. Sometimes at the end of a piece of shaping there are three stitches remaining. The pattern will specify that you knit or purl them together. Do this in the same way as you would when working two stitches together, but insert the right-hand needle through three stitches instead of two. Cut off the yarn and thread through the stitch remaining on the needle in order to fasten off the work.

Decreasing by knitting two stitches together

1 Insert RH needle tip from left to right through front of second stitch on LH needle.

2 Push RH needle farther, taking it from front to back of first stitch on LH needle: the RH needle is now inserted from front to back through first two stitches.

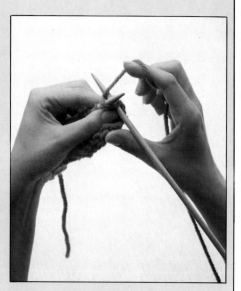

3 Wind yarn under and over RH needle in a clockwise direction.

4 Draw a new stitch through the two loops on the LH needle in the same way as knitting.

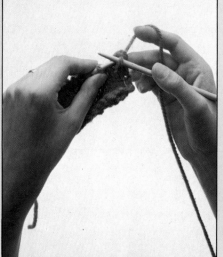

5 Slip the two knitted-together stitches off the LH needle as if knitting a single stitch.

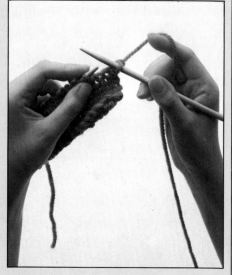

6 The single stitch formed by knitting the first two stitches together is now on the RH needle.
Work to the end of the row as directed in the pattern.

7 To knit three stitches together, insert RH needle from left to right through front of first three stitches on LH needle.

8 Wind the yarn around the RH needle and knit in the usual way, drawing one new stitch through the three loops on the LH needle.
If this is the last stitch in the work, finish as shown at right.

9 Cut off the yarn about 4in (10cm) from the needle. Loosen the remaining stitch on the needle; thread the yarn through and draw the stitch up tightly in the same way as finishing off the last stitch of a bound-off edge.

Decreasing by purling two stitches together

1 Insert RH needle from right to left through front of first two stitches in a purl row.

2 Wind yarn over top and around RH needle in a counterclockwise direction.

3 Use left thumb to gently push RH needle point back through two loops on LH needle in the same way as purling.

4 Twist RH needle upward and forward: there is a new loop on the RH needle and the stitches you are working into remain on the LH needle.

5 Slip the two purled-together stitches off the LH needle as in purling a single stitch.

6 The single stitch formed by purling the first two stitches together is now on the RH needle. Work to the end of the row as directed in the pattern.

Loose and bulky jacket

Wear this loose, open jacket when you need a cover-up on cooler days. It's made from twelve squares pieced together. The intriguing tri-angular effect is achieved by reversing the right and wrong sides of the work half-way through each square.

Sizes
These directions are for the measurements shown on the diagram. The jacket is very loose and fits bust sizes from 32½ to 36in (83 to 92cm).

Materials
25oz (700g) of a bulky yarn
1 pair of Nos. 9 (6mm) and 10 (6½mm) knitting needles

Gauge
13sts and 16 rows to 4in (10cm) over stockinette st on No. 10 (6½mm) needles.

To make square
Using No. 10 (6½mm) needles cast on 3 sts.
☐ Inc one st, K to end of row. Inc one st, P to end of row. Inc one st, K to last st of 3rd row, inc one st. Inc one st, P to last st of 4th row, inc one st. There are now 9sts.
☐ Repeat these 4 rows 6 times more, then the first and 2nd rows again. There are now 47 sts.
☐ P2 tog, P to end of row. This P row reverses the stockinette st pattern. K2 tog, K to end of row. P2 tog, P to last 2 sts, P2 tog. K2 tog, K to last 2 sts, K2 tog.
☐ Repeat the last 4 rows 6 times more, then the first 2 again. There are now 3sts. P these 3 sts tog. Fasten off yarn. Make 12 squares in all.

To finish
Block each piece so that it measures 10in (25cm) square. Press lightly, taking care not to destroy the texture.
☐ Overcast the squares together, positioning them as shown in diagram, leaving open neck and front as indicated by dotted lines. Press seams carefully.
☐ Join x to xx to form underarm seams and y to yy to form side seams.

Borders
Using No. 9 (6mm) needles cast on 4 sts.
☐ Always slipping first st of every row, work in garter st until strip fits around neck edge, beginning and ending at center front opening. Bind off.
☐ Make a similar border to fit around lower edge. Using overcasting, sew on borders: reverse seam on front neck edges, sewing together on right side of work. Make the borders to fit up the front edges.
☐ Sew front borders in position, reversing seam for 6¼in (16cm) at top edge. Make borders for lower edges of sleeves: join ends of border to form a circle and sew in position.

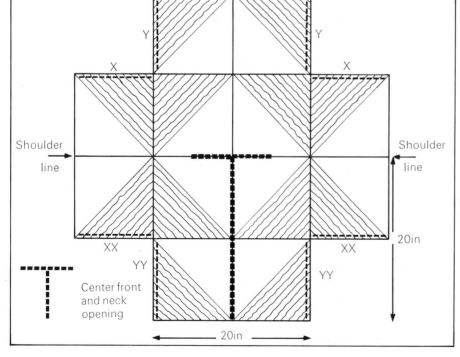

Shoulder line

Shoulder line

20in

Center front and neck opening

20in

John Hawkins

*Duplicate stitch embroidery
*Following a duplicate stitch chart
*Designing your own motif or pattern
*Pattern for a picture sweater

Duplicate stitch embroidery

An effective way to work colored patterns into ordinary knitting is to embroider them in duplicate stitch — it is easy to do and avoids the complications of working with different colored yarns while you are knitting. Work it before the garment pieces are sewn together.

All kinds of designs are suitable — you could try anything from numbers and names to a rose in full bloom. Use it to bring a forgotten old sweater back to life or make use of the extra thickness to strengthen the places that get a lot of wear and tear, such as elbows.

A solid fabric such as one in stockinette stitch is the best background — as you embroider, each knitted stitched is individually covered with a new color, so that the finished result looks just like the original knitting, but the embroidered area is double the thickness. Choose a yarn of the same thickness as the background — don't try to cover a thick yarn with a thinner one or vice versa.

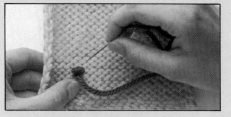

1 Thread a large blunt-ended needle with yarn. Secure yarn by working two or three stitches on top of each other on the back of the first stitch at lower right-hand (RH) corner of the motif — the left-hand (LH) side of fabric when you are working on the back.

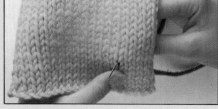

2 Insert the needle from the back to the front of the work through the base of the first stitch.

3 On the front of the fabric, thread the needle from right to left under the two vertical loops of the same stitch, but one row above.

4 Pull the yarn through. A stitch is formed, covering the RH vertical loop of the knitted stitch. (Don't pull the yarn too tight; the embroidery must be kept at the gauge of the background.)

5 Re-insert the needle into the base of the stitch you are covering and out to the front again through the base of the next stitch to the left.

6 Pull the yarn through. A stitch is formed covering the LH vertical loop of the knitted stitch; one duplicate stitch is now complete.

7 To complete the first line of the block of color, continue working from right to left along a row, repeating steps 3 to 6 for the number of stitches required. Finish with the needle at the base of the work.

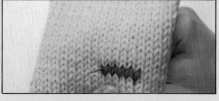

8 To work the row above when the LH edge of the block is a straight line, insert the needle from the back to the front through the center of the last stitch worked.

9 It is easier to work even-numbered rows if you turn the knitting upside down. On the the front of the fabric, thread the needle under the two vertical loops of the same stitch, but one row below.

Paul Williams

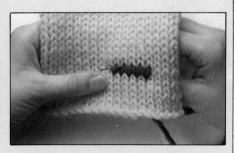

10 Embroider the stitch in the usual way. To work the next stitch bring the needle to the front of the fabric, through the base of the next stitch to the left. Continue in this way until you come to the end of the row. Turn your work the other way up before beginning the next row.

11 If the first embroidered stitch of the second row is located one stitch to the left, begin the row by re-inserting the needle through the center of the next unworked stitch at the end of the first row.

12 To move the first stitch of the second row one stitch to the right, re-insert the needle through the center of the second to last embroidered stitch on the first row.

Following a duplicate stitch chart

Sometimes a knitting pattern will include a selection of motifs that can be duplicate stitched on the garment. These motifs are usually shown in chart form, on a graph. Each square on the graph represents an individual stitch. Each horizontal line of squares represents a row of knitting; each vertical line, the number of rows. On some charts the different colors are indicated by various symbols — circles, crosses and so on.

Another method of showing the different colors is for the chart to be printed with the actual colors to be used, leaving the background grid visible, so that you can check the number of stitches and rows. Do not be misled by charts on graph paper. Knitted stitches are not square; most stitches are wider than they are tall, so that the design on graph paper looks wider and shorter when you transfer it to the garment. To see the design as it will

look on your knitting you will have to draw your own grid representing the stitches in their actual proportion, then block in the design on you new grid. Before you begin embroidering with duplicate stitch find the correct position for the design on the garment. Some patterns specify an exact spot; otherwise, mark where you want the center of the design to be and locate your first stitch from that point.

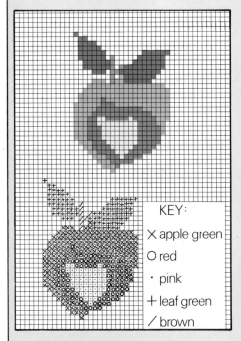

KEY:
X apple green
O red
· pink
+ leaf green
/ brown

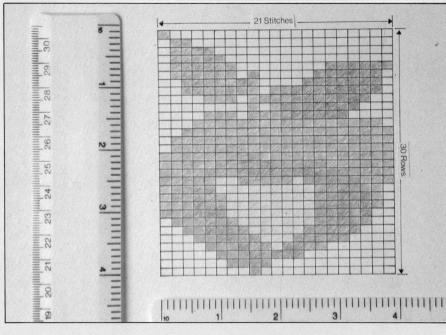

1 The design to be embroidered is usually printed in chart form in either of these two ways: one uses symbols to represent the colors and the other has the appropriate colors on the background grid.

2 To see what the design will look like on your knitting, draw a grid showing the stitches in proportion. This grid is based on a fabric that has 21 stitches and 30 rows to 4in (10cm).

3 Color in the design exactly from the squared chart. The true proportions of your finished design are now visible. If the design flattens too much you can add extra rows to make it taller.

continued

Paul Williams

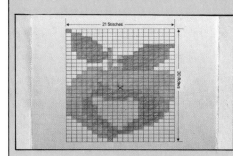

4 Mark the center of the design so that you can position it correctly on the knitting. Note that the lower RH corner of the area occupied by the motif is located 10 stitches across to the right and 14 rows down.

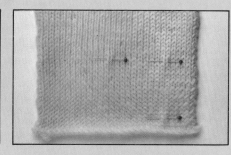

5 Mark the approximate center stitch in the area of knitting that you are embroidering. Count the necessary number of stitches across and rows down to the right to mark the lower RH corner of the area on the fabric.

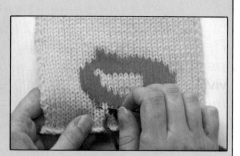

6 When you finish a block in the first color, work an adjacent block in another color. Don't be tempted to work all the blocks in the same color first: it is easy to lose your place if you make isolated islands of color.

Designing you own motif or pattern

For a really personal look, design your own motif or pattern. Use your own drawing or a picture from a book as reference, but remember to keep it simple. It is usually difficult to represent fine details with duplicate stitch and the degree of detail possible depends on the type of yarn used for the background fabric. Fine sport yarns have more stitches and rows to a certain measurement than knitting worsted or bulky yarns. This will give you more scope for details. Check the number of stitches and rows which are available in the area that you want to embroider — and beware of drawing a chart that has many more stitches and rows than you will actually have room for.

1 Find a simple stylized drawing or transfer for an embroidery design. Remember that the type of fabric you are embroidering dictates the amount of detail you can depict. In general don't attempt too detailed a design.

2 Transfer the main outlines to tracing paper. Think in terms of areas of color rather than linear detail.

3 Place carbon paper shiny side down on a piece of graph paper. Position the tracing paper on top of the carbon and pencil over the outlines of the design, transferring them to the graph paper.

4 Go over the outline, deciding as it passes through each square whether to include that stitch in the embroidery. When the outline divides a square, and the greater part of the square is within the design, include the whole square in the design. Use a pencil for the outline at this stage so that you can amend it if necessary.

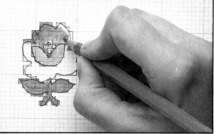

5 Lightly color in the design so that you can see the background grid: this enables you to count the stitches and rows in each block of color.

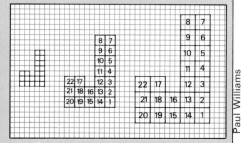

6 This simple stylized design has been enlarged to two and three times the original size. To do this replace each square in the original chart with four squares for twice the size — nine for three times the size — arranged to form a square block. The symmetry of the design is maintained.

Paul Williams

Picture a sweater

Here's proof that a simple sweater does not have to be plain. Knit these sweaters in vivid colors, then decorate them in easy-to-work duplicate stitch embroidery.

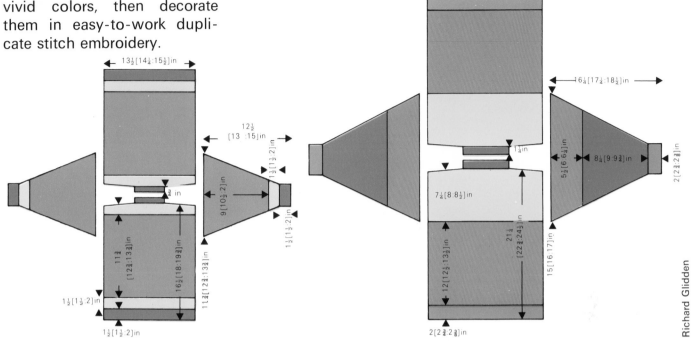

Richard Glidden

Sizes
Directions are for the measurements shown on the diagrams.
To fit a 26[28:30:32½:34:36]in (66[71:76:83:87:92]cm) chest/bust.
Note that directions for larger sizes are in brackets []: where there is only one set of figures it applies to all sizes.

Materials
9[11:13:15:16:18]oz (250[300:350:400:450:500]g) of sport yarn
Child's sweater uses 6[8:9]oz (150[200:250]g) of blue
2[4:4]oz (50[100:100]g) each of yellow and green
Adult's sweater uses 8[8:9]oz (200[200:250]g) of pink
4[4:6]oz (100[100:150]g) each of yellow and green
2[2:4]oz (50[50:100]g) of blue
1 pair each Nos. 4 (3½mm) and 5 (4mm) knitting needles

Gauge
22 sts and 30 rows to 4in (10cm) in stockinette st.
Back and front (alike)
Using No 4 (3½mm) needles and green [green:green:blue:blue:blue] cast on 75[81:87:93:99:105] sts.
□ **1st rib row** K first st, then P one st and K one st alternately to the end of the row.
□ **2nd rib row** P first st, then K one st and P one st alternately to the end of the row.
□ Repeat these two rows for 1½[1½:2:2:2⅜:2⅜]in (4[4:5:5:6:6]cm) ending with a 2nd rib row.

Kim Sayer

41

Above, a set of numbers for you to copy; enlarge if necessary.
Below, motif for the child's sweater (not taken from above set).

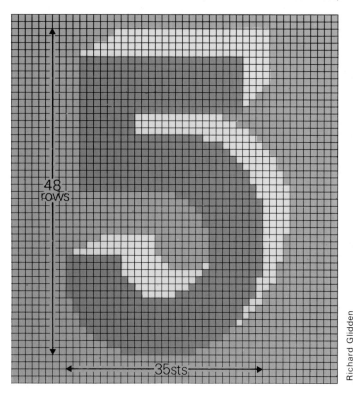

48 rows

35sts

Richard Glidden

Kim Sayer

☐ Change to No. 5 (4mm) needles. Beginning with a K row, proceed in stockinette st working in colors as shown on diagram for the size you are making, until work measures $16\frac{1}{2}[18:19\frac{3}{4}:21\frac{1}{4}:22\frac{3}{4}:24\frac{1}{2}]$ in (42[46:50:54:58:62] cm) from cast-on edge, ending with a P row.

☐ Shape shoulders by binding off 6[7:7:8:8:9] sts at the beginning of next 4 rows and 6[6:8:8:10:10] sts at the beginning of following 2 rows. 39[41:43:45:47:49] sts.

☐ Change to No. 4 needles ($3\frac{1}{2}$mm) and work the 2 rib rows for $\frac{3}{4}[\frac{3}{4}:\frac{3}{4}:1\frac{1}{4}:1\frac{1}{4}:1\frac{1}{4}]$ in (2[2:2:3:3:3]cm) for neck band.

☐ Bind off loosely in rib.

Sleeves (make 2)

using No. 4 ($3\frac{1}{2}$mm) needles and green [green:green:blue:blue:blue] cast on 35 [39:43:47:51:55] sts. Work the 2 rib rows of back and front for $1\frac{1}{2}[1\frac{1}{2}:2:2:2\frac{3}{4}:2\frac{3}{8}]$in (4[4:5:5:6:6]cm), ending with a 2nd rib row.

☐ Change to No. 5 (4mm) needles. Beginning with a K row, proceed in stockinette st working in colors as shown on the diagram for the size you are making, increasing one st at each end of next and every following 6th row until there are 65[71:77:83:89:95] sts.

☐ Now work straight until sleeve measures $12\frac{1}{2}[13\frac{3}{4}:15:16\frac{1}{4}:17\frac{1}{4}:18\frac{1}{2}]$in (32 [35:38:41:44:47]cm) from cast-on edge, ending with a P row. Bind off loosely.

To finish

Do not press.

☐ Darn in all ends on the wrong side.

☐ With right sides of back and front together, join shoulder and neckband seams using a backstitch seam.

☐ Embroider motifs as shown in charts.

☐ Mark center of bound-off edge of sleeves with a pin. Fold front and back sections with right sides together, match pin to shoulder seam and pin bound-off edge along side edges of main piece. Sew on sleeves with backstitch seam.

☐ With right sides together, join side and sleeve seams, joining waistbands and cuffs with a flat seam and the remainder with a backstitch seam.

Kim Sayer

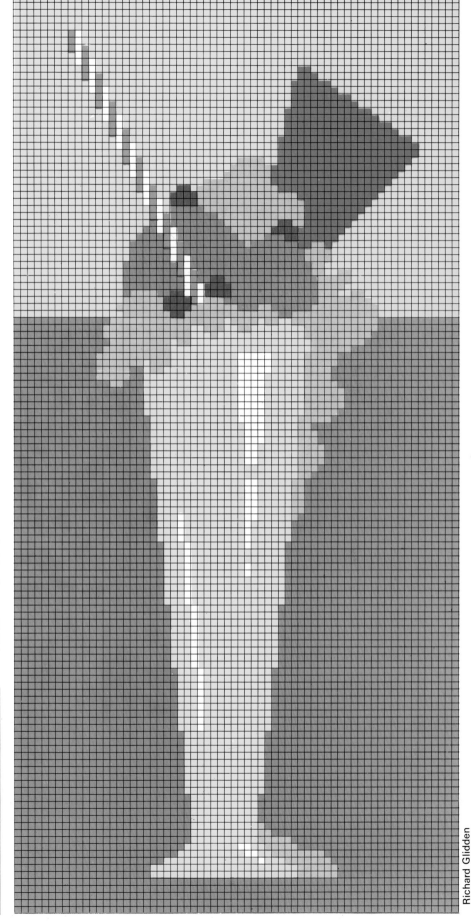

Richard Glidden

Sewing / COURSE 7

*Understitching
*Front hip pocket
*Applying a zipper
*Pattern for a gathered skirt with front hip pockets: directions for making (1)

Understitching

Understitching is used to hold the facing to the seam allowance to prevent it from rolling over the seam edge. It is done on the inside edge of the facing or undersection and does not show on the right side.

Use it on neckline edges, openings, faced edges, collars, cuffs and pockets. Do it after applying the facing to the garment or the undercollar to the top collar.

1 Apply the facing, pressing the seam allowance toward the facing.

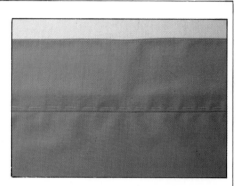

2 Baste the seam allowance to the facing so that it is held firmly in position.

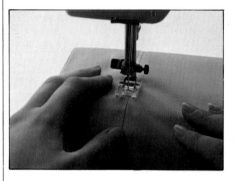

3 On the right side, stitch through both the facing and the seam allowance close to the seamline of the facing.

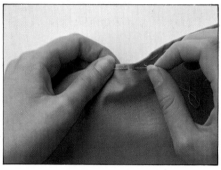

4 Turn facing to the inside and, with the right side on top, baste close to the stitched edge, slightly rolling the seam to the wrong side as you do so.

5 Press the stitched edge flat.

Applying a front hip pocket

For a good-looking pocket that is really functional a front hip pocket is ideal—it can be used both on skirts and pants and can be left plain or finished with topstitching, binding or braid.

The pocket is stitched to the garment first and then incorporated into the side seam.

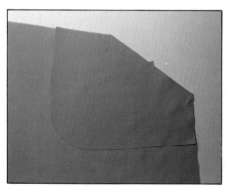

1 With right sides together, matching notches and circles, pin and baste pocket facings to skirt front.

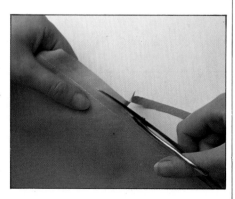

2 Stitch the seam. Grade the seam allowance by trimming the facing allowance to $\frac{1}{4}$in (6mm) and the garment allowance to $\frac{3}{8}$in (1 cm).

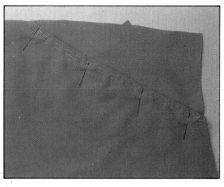

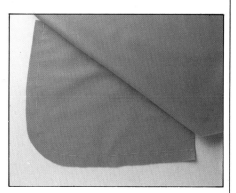

3 Understitch the seam allowance to the pocket facing. Turn the facing to the underside, and baste close to edge.

4 With the right side of the pocket piece and skirt front facing upward, place skirt front over pocket pieces, matching circles at the waistline and side seams. Pin and baste in place.

5 On the inside of the skirt front, pin and baste the pocket pieces to the pocket facings around the outer edges.

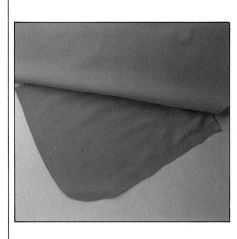

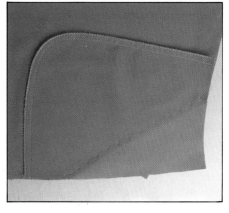

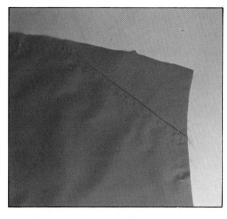

6 With the pocket piece on top, stitch around pocket, starting at the waistline and stitching around to the side edge.

7 To finish the outer edge of pocket, overcast or machine zig-zag the raw edges together. Press.

8 Baste the pockets to skirt at waistline and side edges.

Applying a zipper by the lapped-seam method

Although zippers may be applied for decoration, they are usually meant to be inconspicuous fastenings. The best way to conceal a zipper is to sew it in by hand, and this method should always be used on fine fabrics. But you can also apply a zipper by machine, using the zipper foot. In either case, it is advisable to insert the zipper early in the making of the garment, when you have a flat seam to work with and less bulk to handle.

Whether you apply a zipper by hand or by machine, you have a choice of several methods of inserting it. The lapped-seam method is a good standard way of putting in a zipper so that the teeth are concealed. It can be used on any part of the garment.

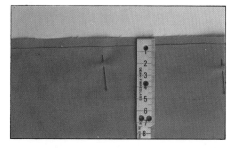

1 When cutting out the garment allow $\frac{1}{4}$in (5mm) extra seam allowance on the underlap edge. This will be on the back of the garment for a side opening and on the left side for a center back or center front opening.

2 With right sides together, matching seamlines, baste and stitch the seam up to the zipper opening. The underlap seam allowance will extend $\frac{1}{4}$in (5mm) beyond the overlap seam allowance. Snip the Underlap seam allowance to within $\frac{1}{4}$in (5mm) of the stitching line. Press seam open and trim the underlap seam below zipper opening to $\frac{5}{8}$in (1.5cm).

continued

Paul Williams

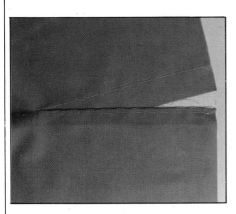

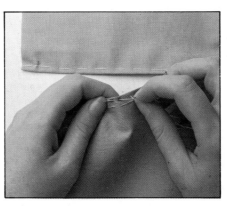

3 Turn under and baste the overlap seam allowance close to the folded edge.

4 Turn under the underlap seam allowance $\frac{1}{4}$in (5mm) beyond the seamline and baste close to folded edge.

5 Press basted edges flat.

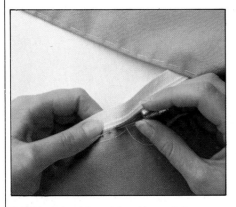

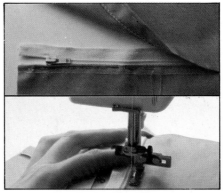

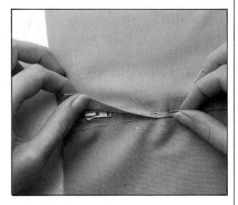

6 With right sides of the skirt and zipper facing up, position zipper behind the underlap with folded edge of seam close to zipper teeth. Baste zipper in place.

7 Stitch by machine, using zipper foot.
8 Alternatively, using a tiny backstitch, with the stitches placed slightly apart (called prickstitch), sew the garment to the zipper close to the folded edge, beginning at the bottom of the zipper and working toward the top.

9 Place the overlap over zipper so that the folded edge continues along the seamline; baste in place.
10 Sew the overlap in place using prickstitch, beginning at the bottom of the zipper at the seamline and working across to the other side of the zipper and up along the side, just beyond the teeth.

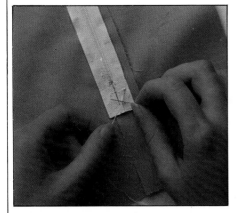

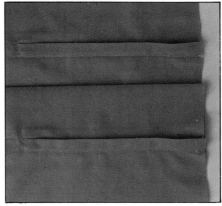

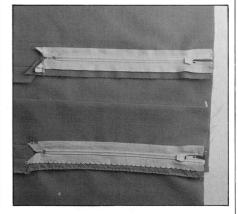

11 Alternatively, stitch by machine, using zipper foot.
12 Pull threads through to wrong side and secure ends. Press lightly on the wrong side.

These two photographs show the finished effect, stitched by hand and by machine.

13 On the wrong side, turn under the lower ends of the zipper tape diagonally and pin. Trim off excess tape.
14 Hem the zipper tape to the seam allowance only. This prevents the tape from rolling up and catching in the zipper teeth.

Gathered skirt:
directions for making (1)

Make this softly gathered skirt in lightweight tweed for a casual look or in a solid-color crepe to accentuate its soft lines. Directions for completing the skirt are in the next sewing course.

Measurement
The pattern is given in sizes 10–20; corresponding to sizes 8–18 in ready-made clothes.
The finished lengths are 28½in (72.5cm), 29in (73.5cm), 29⅜in (74.5cm), 30in (76cm), 30½in (77.5cm), and 31in (79cm), Seam allowance, ⅝in (1.5cm).

Suggested fabrics
Lightweight wool, cottons, crepe.

Materials
36in (90cm)-wide fabric with or without nap
Size 10:2⅝yd (2.4m)
Size 12:2⅞yd (2.6m)
Size 14:3yd (2.7m)
size 16:3⅛yd (2.8m)
Sizes 18 and 20:3¼yd (2.9m)
45in (115cm)-wide fabric with or without nap
Sizes 10, 12 and 14:2⅜yd (2.1m)
Sizes 16, 18 and 20:2½yd (2.2m)
54in (1.40cm)-wide fabric without nap
Sizes 10 and 12:1⅝yd (1.4m)
Size 14:1¾yd (1.5m)
Sizes 16 and 18:1¾yd (1.6m)
Size 20:2yd (1.8m)
36in (90cm)-wide interfacing fabric
Sizes 10 to 18:¼yd (20cm)
Size 20:⅜yd (30cm)
Matching thread
7in (18cm) skirt zipper; Hook and eye

Key to pattern pieces

1 Skirt front   Cut 1 on fold
2 Skirt back   Cut 2
3 Pocket facing   Cut 2
4 Pocket piece   Cut 2
5 Waistband   Cut 1
Interfacing: use piece 5

1 Cut out the pattern pieces from the pattern sheet, following the correct line for the size you want. The patterns for the skirt front and back are each in two pieces and must be joined before you lay them on the fabric.
2 Prepare the fabric and pin on the pattern pieces, following the layouts given. Make sure that you place the grain lines along the correct grain of the fabric. Cut out the pieces, following the edges of the pattern closely.
3 Transfer all the pattern marks.

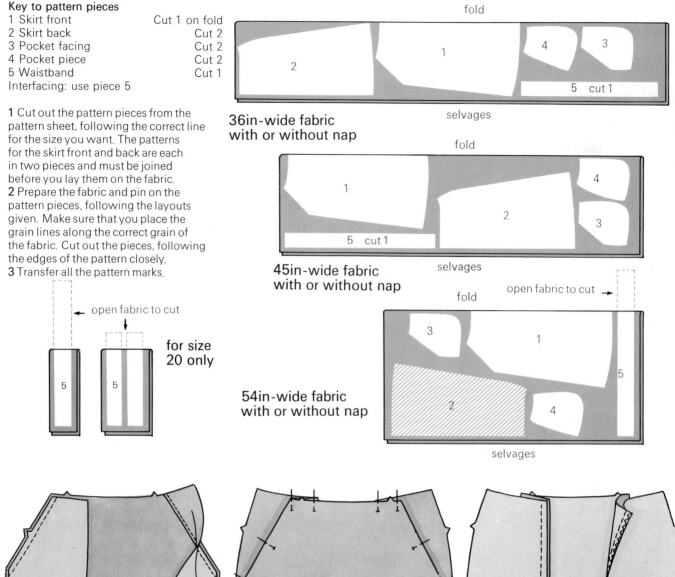

36in-wide fabric
with or without nap

45in-wide fabric
with or without nap

54in-wide fabric
with or without nap

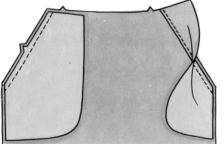

for size
20 only

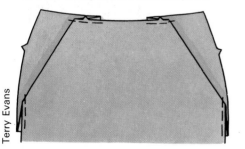

4 With right sides together, matching circles and notches, baste and stitch pocket facings to skirt front; grade seam allowances and understitch to the facing. Turn the facing to the inside and press.

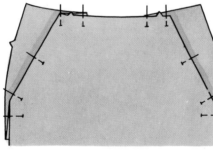

5 Place the skirt front over the pocket pieces, matching circles.

6 On the inside baste and stitch the pocket facing to the pocket piece around the outer edges. Finish the outer edges of the pockets and press.

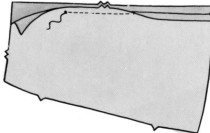

7 Baste pockets to the skirt front at waist and side edges.

8 With right sides together, matching notches, baste and stitch the center back seam as far as the circle.

9 Insert zipper into center back opening, using the lapped-seam method. Directions for completing the skirt are given in the next course.

Terry Evans

Ron Kelly/Blouse and cotton knit top Bobos; shoes by Bally

Catch-stitching interfacing to a garment section

This is a fairly loose but secure stitch, used to hold edges of interfacings to the main fabric. The stitches should not show on the right side of the fabric, and they must not be pulled up tightly or they will pucker.

To ensure that the interfacing lies flat on the fabric, the stitch should be worked with the garment section lying flat on a work surface.

1 Baste interfacing to wrong side of garment section.

2 Start with a double backstitch $\frac{1}{8}$in (3mm) in from the interfacing edge, then pick up a thread of the main fabric diagonally $\frac{1}{8}$in (3mm) above. Pick up the interfacing and the fabric alternately. When picking up the interfacing do not go through to the main fabric. Do not pull the stitches tightly.

Applying a waistband to a gathered skirt

A waistband should fit snugly at the natural waistline without being either too tight or too loose. For a woman's garment it should lap right over left to fasten at center front or center back opening. If the opening is at the side, the front laps over the back. The extension of a waistband lies underneath the other end when fastened. Usually, a waistband is closed with hooks and eyes or a button and buttonhole. Interfacing gives a waistband body and prevents it from stretching out of shape while being worn.

1 With right sides together, matching notches, pin the skirt to the waistband at the center back, side seams and center front. The inside of the skirt should be facing outward, with the waistband inside.

2 Pull up the gathering threads on the skirt so that it fits the waistband. Secure ends of thread around a pin. Spread gathers evenly and pin the skirt to waistband at short intervals.

3 Baste the skirt to waistband and stitch with the skirt on top.

4 Remove the basting and gathering threads. Trim interfacing close to the stitching and grade the seam allowance. Press the seam allowance towards the waistband.

5 Fold waistband, right sides together, along foldline. Baste and stitch across the ends of the waistband.

Paul Williams

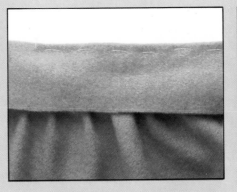

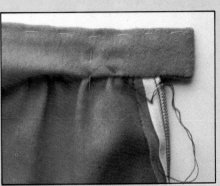

6 Trim interfacing close to stitching. Cut across the corners to reduce thickness.

7 Turn the waistband right side out and baste close to folded edge.

8 On the inside, turn under the seam allowance of the waistband and hem the waistband to the stitching, enclosing seam allowance at waistline. Press.

Buttonhole stitch

Besides being used on hand-sewn buttonholes, this stitch may also be used where a decorative—for example, on cutwork—is needed. It is also used to attach hooks and eyes and for French bar tacks where a hard-wearing, strong stitch is needed.

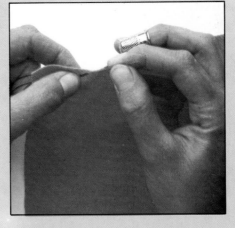

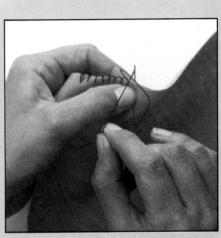

1 Begin by making a double backstitch into the work, then bring the needle to the right side.

2 Insert the needle into the fabric from back to front taking up the required amount. Take the thread across the needle from right to left.

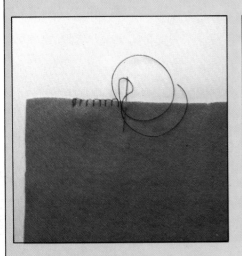

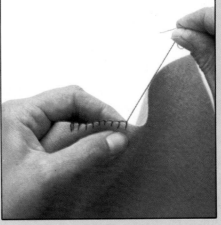

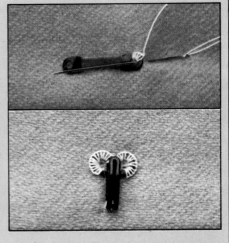

3 Pass the thread under the needle from left to right.

4 Pull the needle through, giving it a gentle tug to form a tiny knot to lie on the edge of the fabric.

5 When sewing on a hook or eye with buttonhole stitch, work the stitches closely around the wire so that the knots lie around the outside of each hole.

Paul Williams

Hooks and eyes

A hook and eye fastening is most often used on a waistband, but can also be used as an additional fastening combined with buttons or a zipper at the top of a neckline for added strength. There are various types and sizes of hooks and eyes. The straight bar eye section is used when the edges of an opening overlap, and the round eye is used when the edges just meet. Skirt and pants hooks and eyes are much larger and stronger then ordinary ones and are more suitable for closing the waistband on medium and heavyweight fabrics.

1 mark the positions of the hook and eye on the waistband. The hook is sewn to the inside of the overlap.

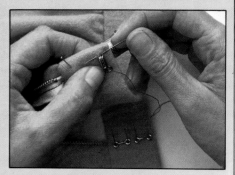

2 Begin with a double backstitch and place the hook in position. Work three to four stitches inside the top of the hook to secure in place.

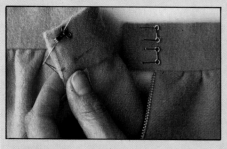

3 Bring the needle down through the fabric and out through one of the holes.

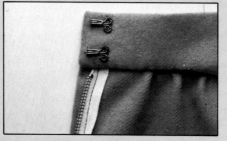

4 Buttonhole stitch around each hole.

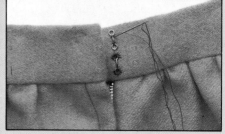

5 Catch the bar or eye to the garment with three or four stitches close to the hole. Sew around holes as for hook.

Ron Kelly/Bouse by Fenn Wright & Manson; shoes by Bally

Gathered skirt with front hip pockets: directions for making (2)

In the last sewing course we gave the first set of directions for the gathered skirt—now we show you how to complete it and add all the finishing touches.

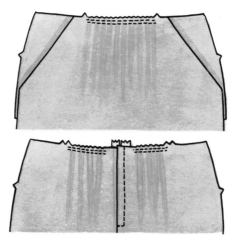

1 Run two rows of gathering stitches between the notches on the front and back waistline of skirt.

2 With right sides together and matching notches, baste and stitch the side seams of skirt. Finish seams and press open.

Terry Evans

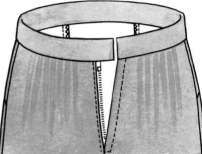

3 For the larger size the waistband interfacing has to be cut in two pieces and joined at the center front to make the complete length of the waistband. Before basting the interfacing to the waistband, overlap the two pieces by ¼in (5mm) at the center front and catch-stitch together to hold.

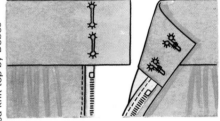

4 Gather the front and back waistline of the skirt to fit the waistband and apply the skirt to the waistband as shown on page 50.

5 Sew hooks and bars to waistband at opening, placing the hooks on the inside of the overlap and the bars on the right side of the underlap or extension.

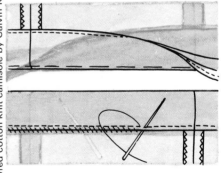

6 Try the skirt on and mark the hem. Turn the hem up and baste close to the folded edge. Trim hem to an even width. Finish the raw edge of the hem by turning in ¼in (5mm) and machine stitching. Sew hem to skirt using hemming stitch. Press the folded edge.

Ron Kelly/Wine-colored cotton knit camisole by Calvin Klein; cream textured knit top by Bobos

Terry Evans

53

Watch this pretty Indian princess disappear into her fabric cone. But she'll rise again at your command.

Ameena, the Puppet Princess

Materials
Piece of printed fabric for dress
  16×8in (40×20cm)
Piece of plain fabric for sleeves
  4×3in (10×8cm)
11in (28cm) square of printed fabric
  for cone
11in (28cm) square of self-adhesive
  paper stiffening for cone
Short pieces of dark brown yarn
Scraps of brown and blue felt
Piece of rust felt 13×2in (33×5cm)
1in (2.5cm)-diameter wooden bead
24in (60cm) of ¼in (5mm)-diameter
  dowel
Scrap of thin gold trimming
Piece of cardboard 5½in (14cm) wide
Black and red felt-tipped pens
Fabric glue; thread

Gary Warren

1 Cut the fabric for the dress into two 8in (20cm) squares. Fold one square in half. Place folded edge at the right and mark a diagonal line from lower left-hand corner to a point 1½in (4cm) from the folded edge. Cut along this line. Repeat on second square to make other side of dress.
2 Cut the sleeve fabric into two rectangles, each 3×2in (8×5cm). Fold each sleeve in half widthwise with right sides together; pin, baste and sew the edge opposite the fold, taking ¼in (5mm) seams.
3 From medium brown felt cut out four mitt-shaped hands. Place pieces together in pairs and topstitch close to edge.
4 Turn in ¼in (5mm) along one open end of each sleeve; gather this edge. Place hands inside gathered sleeve ends; pull up gathers. Sew hands to sleeves.
5 Place the raw edges of sleeves on the side edges of one dress piece (right side of dress up) ⅜in (1cm) from the upper edge, with hands in the center, thumbs pointing up. Lay second dress piece— with right side down—on top. Sew the side seams, including the sleeves, taking a ¼in (5mm) seam.
6 Turn in ¼in (5mm) at neck edge and run a line of gathering stitches around the neck, close to folded edge.
7 For hair, wind yarn around a piece of cardboard over and over. Backstitch along loops of yarn at one edge of cardboard. Hold the bead "head" with the hole vertical, and apply glue to top and back areas. Glue hair in place, so that backstitching makes center part. Leave to dry.

8 Push dowel through neck edge of dress and push firmly into center hole of head. Pull up the gathering thread around the neck of the dress and secure it around the dowel at the base of the head. Fasten a piece of gold trimming around the neck, covering the stitches.
9 Draw the features on the face, using felt-tipped pens.
10 Plait the hair together at the back of the head. Fasten with gold trimming.
11 From rust and blue felt cut out a tiny flower and center. Glue to side of head.
12 On paper stiffening, draw one quarter of a circle, with a 10in (25cm) radius.

Glue to center of cone fabric. Trim fabric allowing a ⅜in (1cm) margin outside the paper. Turn fabric over edges and glue in place.
13 Fold stiffened fabric into a cone shape, overlapping side edges by ⅝in (1.5cm). Slip stitch edges together.
14 Slip the cone on the dowel through neck of cone, so that widest part is at the top. Slip stitch edge of dress to inside edge of cone, easing in the fullness.
15 Using pinking shears, cut out two strips of rust felt to fit cone top and bottom. Glue strips in place over cone edges, overlapping short edges at seam.

Adjusting a pants pattern to fit correctly

The sewing techniques involved in making pants are relatively simple; the problem, usually, is getting the pants to fit correctly. Patterns generally conform to the measurements of a standard figure, and it is often necessary to alter a pattern to accommodate individual figure proportion. Pants entail special fitting problems because of the complexity of the proportions involved. It is important that all major alterations be made on the pattern before the pants are cut out. If there are a number of fitting problems, it is advisable to test the pattern by making it in muslin first. Once all problems have been solved and a perfect fit achieved, this basic pattern may be adapted for all kinds of pants.

Waistline adjustment

1 The ease allowance at the waistline should be $\frac{5}{8}$–$\frac{3}{4}$in (1.5–2cm). The waistline can be increased or decreased by adjusting the darts. Each dart can be increased or decreased by as much as $\frac{1}{4}$in (5mm), but no more. Do not alter the length of the dart.

2 If this adjustment is not sufficient the side seams can also be altered. Divide the amount of the increase or decrease by four, and adjust each side seam by this amount. Taper to the hipline; take care not to change the hip measurement.

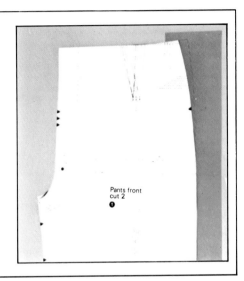

Crotch length

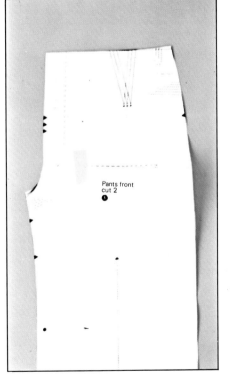

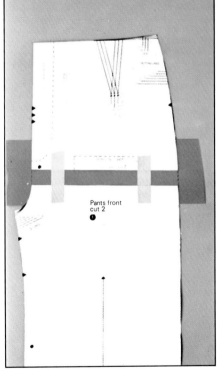

1 To determine the crotch length, sit on a straight chair and measure from the waistline to the seat. To this measurement add $\frac{1}{2}$in (1.3cm) ease if the hips are less than 35in (89cm); $\frac{3}{4}$in (2cm) if the hips are 35in (89cm) to 38in (96.5cm) and 1in (2.5cm) if the hips are more than 38in (96.5cm). The body measurement plus ease allowance is the total crotch length. Any adjustment made to the crotch length must be made to both front and back pattern pieces.

2 To adjust the crotch length, draw a line across the pattern at right angles to the grain line, from crotch point (the sharp angle) to side seam. The pattern length from the waistline to this line should equal total crotch length.

3 If the pattern is too long, fold it along the shortening line to take up the desired amount.

4 Tape the fold in place. Redraw the cutting lines.

5 If the pattern is too short, cut along the lengthening line and open the pattern the desired amount.

6 Insert a piece of paper and tape in place. Redraw the cutting lines.

Paul Williams

Hip and thigh adjustments

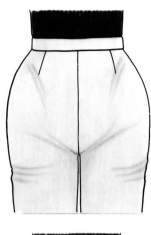

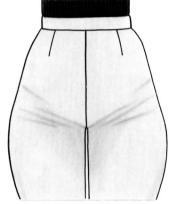

1 Take the hip measurement on the pattern hipline, this being approximately 8in (20.5cm) below the waistline, or at the widest part. There should be 2in (5cm) ease allowance. If the pattern does not measure 2in (5cm) more than the body measurement, the pattern will need adjusting.

2 To increase the hipline, first tape a long piece of paper under the side seam edge of each pattern piece. Divide the extra amount needed by four. Increase each side seam by this amount, measuring out from the hipline at the side edge on front and back pieces and marking the paper extension. Draw a new cutting line, tapering from mark at hipline into the original cutting line above the knee and at the waistline.

3 On some figures the thighs bulge out below the hips. For this problem, alter the pattern in the same way, drawing the extension so that the greatest amount of increase is at the fullest part of the thigh and tapering the line farther down on the leg.

4 To decrease the hipline, use the same principle as above, but subtract the amount at the side seams.

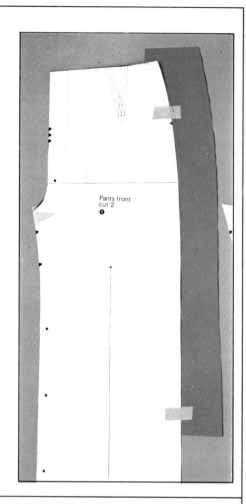

Sway back

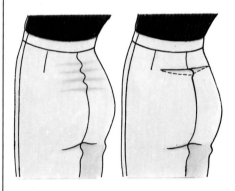

1 If the figure has a sway back this will cause folds in the pants below the back waistline. These folds can be eliminated by removing the extra fullness at the center back. To be sure of taking in the necessary amount of fullness, you should first make up the pattern in muslin and pin a horizontal dart across the back.

2 To decrease the back waist length, slash across the back to the side seam about 3½in (9cm) below the waistline. Overlap the slash line to remove the necessary amount.

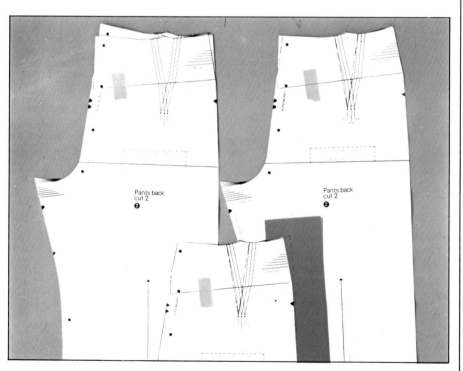

3 Redraw the center back line and the darts if they have been affected.
4 If the normal waist width is required, add the amount trimmed from the center back to the side seam and taper from the waistline to the hipline.

Large stomach

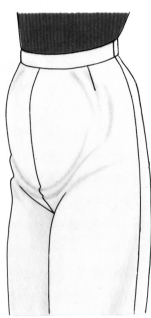

1 If the figure has a large stomach, this will cause folds at each side of the pants.

2 To make this alteration, draw a line through the center of the waistline dart to the knee. This line should be parallel to the grain line. Then draw a horizontal line from the center front to the side seam about 3in (7.5cm) below the waistline. To determine the extra amount required, measure over the stomach from side seam to side seam.

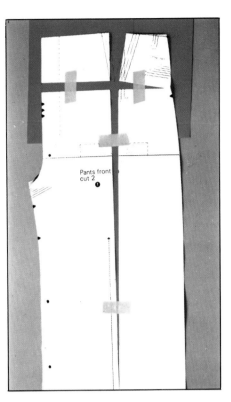

3 Slash the horizontal line to the side seam and open the pattern a quarter of the amount required, the center front being kept straight. Slash the vertical line and open the pattern the same amount, keeping the center front straight. Insert the tape paper under the slashes. Redraw the waistline dart in the middle of the slash, returning it to its original position and size. Smooth out side seam.

Adjusting the width at lower leg

1 If the pant leg at the lower edge is too narrow, divide the extra amount required by four and add this amount to the outside and inside leg seam edges at the hemline. Taper from the hemline to the hipline on the side seams, also from the hemline to the crotch on the inside seams.

2 If the pattern is too wide at this point, use the same method, but subtract the amount at these seams.

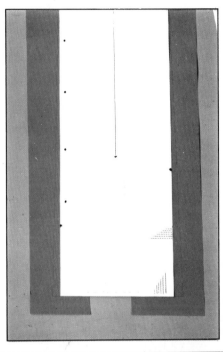

Large buttocks

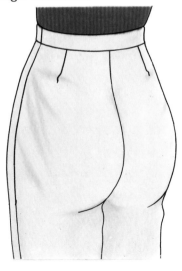

1 Large buttocks will cause folds from the lower seat up toward hipline.

2 To make this alteration you must increase the width and length at the fullest part of the buttocks. Determine amount required by measuring across the fullest part of buttocks from side seam to side seam. Slash the pattern vertically to the knee, between the center back and dart. Measure down from the waistline to the fullest part of buttocks. Slash the pattern horizontally at this point from the center back to the side seam. Open each slash a quarter of the amount required, keeping the center back straight. Insert a piece of paper and tape in place. Redraw the cutting lines. If the waist is now too large, take the extra amount into the dart and, if necessary, off the side seam at the waist.

Note To alter the pattern for a flat bottom slash pattern as above, but overlap the amount to be reduced. If the waist is now too small, add the extra amount to the dart and, if necessary, to the side seam at the waist.

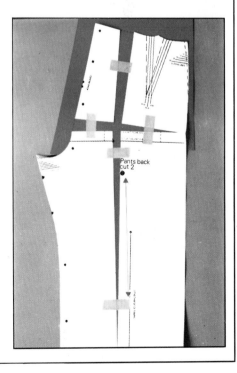

Basic pants: direction for making (1)

The pattern for these smart pants is included in the Stitch by Stitch Pattern Pack. In this chapter we begin the directions for making the pants, and in the next chapter we show you how to complete them. Variations for this and the other patterns in the Pack will be provided in future courses.

Measurements
The pattern is given in sizes 10, 12, 14, 16, 18 and 20, corresponding to sizes 8 to 18 in ready-made clothes. A guide to our sizes is in the front of all volumes.
Finished lengths are 43in (109cm), 43½in (110.5cm), 44in (112cm), 44¾in (113.5cm), 45¼in (115cm) and 46in (116.5cm).

Suggested fabrics
Medium-weight closely woven woolens such as flannel and gabardine; closely woven medium-weight cottons or synthetics.

Materials
36in (90cm) and 45in (115cm)-wide fabric with or without nap
Size 10: 2⅞yd (2.6m)
Size 12: 2⅞yd (2.6m)
Size 14: 2⅞yd (2.6m)
Size 16: 2⅞yd (2.6m)
Size 18: 3yd (2.7m)
Size 20: 3yd (2.7m)

54in (140cm)-wide fabric without nap
Size 10: 1⅝yd (1.4m)
Size 12: 1⅝yd (1.4m)
Size 14: 2⅞yd (2.6m)
Size 16: 2⅞yd (2.6m)
Size 18: 3yd (2.7m)
Size 20: 3yd (2.7m)

Interfacing
36in (90cm)-wide fabric
Sizes 10, 12, 14, 16, 18: ¼yd (20cm)
Size 20: ⅜yd (30cm)

Matching thread
7in (18cm) skirt zipper
Hooks and eyes

Key to pattern pieces
1 Pants front   Cut 2
2 Pants back   Cut 2
3 Waistband   Cut 1
4 Fly facing   Cut 3
Interfacing   Use piece 3.

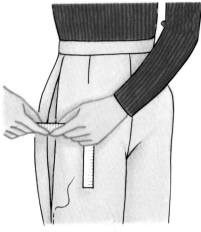

1 Trim each pattern piece to the required size, following the appropriate line marked on each piece. Iron the pieces to remove any crease.

2 Make the necessary alterations in the pattern. If you have difficult fitting problems, such as a sway back or a large stomach, you should first cut out the pants legs and waistband in muslin and baste these pieces together firmly. Then make the necessary adjustments on the muslin version, and use these altered pieces as your pattern for the pants front and back.

3 Prepare the fabric and pin on the pattern pieces following the layouts given. Make sure that you place the pieces with the direction lines on the correct grain of the fabric. Cut out the pieces following closely the edges of the pattern.

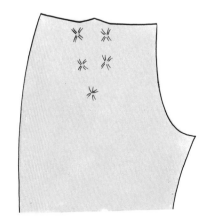

4 Transfer all the pattern marks, using either tailor's chalk on the wrong side or tailor's tacks.

cutting layouts

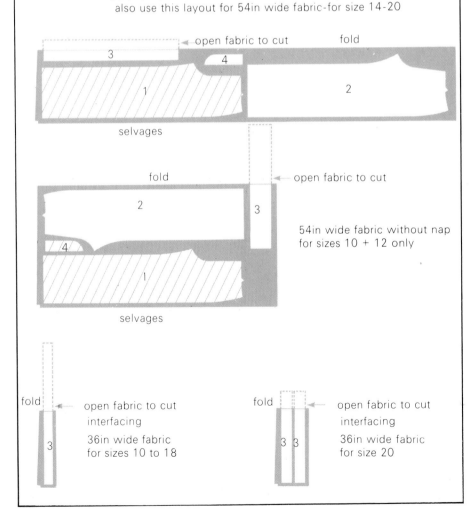

36 and 45in wide fabric with or without nap for all sizes also use this layout for 54in wide fabric-for size 14-20

open fabric to cut   fold

3
4
1
2

selvages

fold   open fabric to cut

2
3
4
1

selvages

54in wide fabric without nap for sizes 10 + 12 only

fold   open fabric to cut
interfacing
36in wide fabric for sizes 10 to 18
3

fold   open fabric to cut
interfacing
36in wide fabric for size 20
3 3

Shoestring

Good old Patch!

Delight a small child with this two-faced patchwork bear. You can use up fabric scraps too, so he's a real penny saver.

Materials

$\frac{1}{8}$yd (.1m) each of six different green printed fabrics, 36in (90cm) wide
$\frac{1}{8}$yd (.1m) each of six different blue printed fabrics, 36in (90cm) wide
Scraps of white, black, red, blue and green felt
matching threads
Two 32in (80cm) pieces of $1\frac{1}{8}$in (3.5cm)-wide ribbon in two contrasting colors
Piece of cardboard 3in (8cm) square
Polyester stuffing, tracing paper

1 Using the square piece of cardboard as a pattern, cut out six patches from each of the different fabrics. Always align the side of the template with the straight grain of the fabric and make sure that each patch is cut out accurately.

2 Arrange the 36 green patches, following the diagram, to give a balanced selection of color and pattern for one side of the bear.

3 Repeat step 2, using blue patches.

4 make each side in the following way: place two adjoining patches with right sides together, edges matching. Pin, baste and stitch along one side, taking $\frac{3}{8}$in (1cm) seam allowance. Press seam open.

5 Join another patch to the first two in the same way, building up a strip. Continue, following the diagram, until both sides of the bear are complete.

6 Place the two sides with right sides together. Pin, baste and stitch all around, taking $\frac{3}{8}$in (1cm) seam allowance and leaving an opening in one side.

7 Clip corners and turn right side out. Stuff bear firmly. Turn in opening edges and slip stitch together.

8 For green side of bear, cut out two $1\frac{3}{4}$in (4.5cm)-diameter circles for outer eyes from white felt. Cut out two $1\frac{1}{4}$in (3.5cm)-diameter circles from green felt for middle eyes. Cut out two 1in (2.5cm)-diameter circles from black felt for pupils.

9 Repeat step 8 to cut out eyes for blue side of the bear, but use blue felt for middle eyes.

10 Using tracing paper, trace and cut out patterns for nose and tongue. Cut out two noses from black felt and two tongues from red felt.

11 Position features on green side of bear, hand-sew in place.

12 Repeat step 11, sewing features on blue side of bear.

13 Cut the two pieces of ribbon in half. Pin, baste and stitch two contrasting pieces of ribbon together at one end. Finish other ends if necessary. Repeat with remaining pieces of ribbon.

14 Sew each ribbon to the side of the bear's head just above each arm, matching ribbon seams with side seams, so ribbons are the same on each side. Tie a bow on each side.

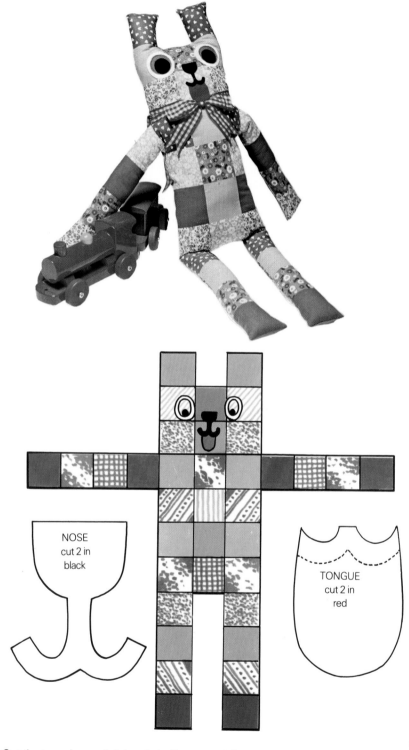

NOSE
cut 2 in
black

TONGUE
cut 2 in
red

Rupert Watts

Terry Evans

*Fly-front zipper
*Blanket stitch
*Bar tack
*Waistline dart
*Pattern for basic pants:
 directions for making (2)

Fly-front zipper

A fly-front zipper is the usual kind of closing for men's trousers, but it is also often used on women's pants, especially in sportswear, as it is neat and strong. The fly front consists of a facing and a fly shield, which is also faced, so you will need to cut out three fly-facing pieces altogether. On men's trousers the fly laps left over right and on a woman's, right over left. Here we give instructions for the women's version. For men's — or unisex — trousers, reverse directions.

Zippers in fly-front closings should always be stitched by machine for strength. Use a zipper foot on the machine so that the stitching may be worked close to the edge of the zipper teeth.

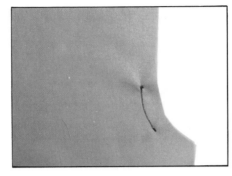

1 With right sides together, baste and stitch the front crotch seam from circle to within 1⅜in (3.5cm) of inside leg seam. Clip curve and press seam open.

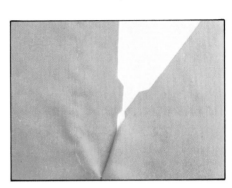

2 On the right front mark the curve of topstitching with basting.

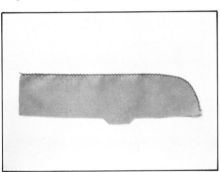

3 Finish curved edge of one fly-facing piece by hand or machine overcasting

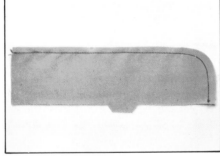

4 With right sides together, baste and stitch the other two fly-facing pieces together on the curved edge, taking a ¼in (5mm) seam allowance.

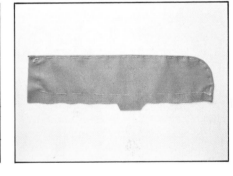

5 Grade the seam allowance, turn shield right side out and baste close to stitched edge and along seam-lines on raw edges. Press flat.

6 With right sides together, matching notches, baste and stitch the fly facing to the right center front, stitching from the circle to the waistline.

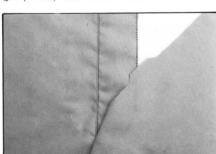

7 Press the seam allowance toward the facing and understitch the facing to seam allowance, stitching close to the seamline. Press.

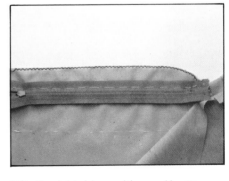

8 On the right side, position and baste zipper face down to the facing, with the left edge of zipper tape along the facing seam and the lower edge of zipper ⅜in (1cm) from lower edge of opening.

continued

Paul Williams

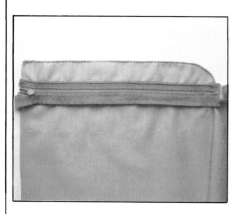

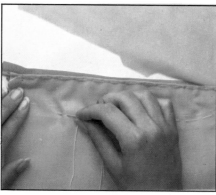

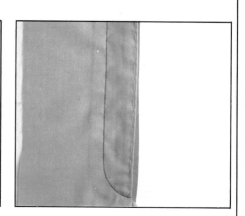

9 With the zipper foot on the machine, stitch the right side of the zipper tape to the facing, as close to the teeth as possible. Work a second row of machine stitching close to the zipper tape edge.

10 Fold the facing and zipper to the inside of the pants along the seamline and baste close to the seam edge and then along the curved edge of facing.

11 On the right side, work a row of top-stitching to hold the facing in place, using the first row of basting as a guide. Stitch from the circle or lower edge to the waistline, keeping the end of unstitched left zipper tape free. Trim the left front seam allowance to stitching.

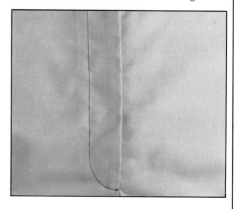

12 Turn under the seam allowance at the center front of the left-hand side and baste in place. Press. Working with the zipper open, place the left front over the zipper tape close to the teeth and baste together.

13 With the right side facing up, baste the fly shield to the left front behind zipper, matching the seam edges on the wrong side. With the zipper foot on the machine, stitch the zipper and facing in place, stitching from the right side, close to the zipper teeth.

14 To strengthen the lower edge of the opening, work a small bar tack across the bottom of the zipper opening, using blanket stitch.

Blanket stitch

Often used in embroidery, blanket stitch is also used in sewing to finish raw edges and to make bar tacks. For a bar tack, the stitch is worked over a foundation bar of threads. This stitch differs from button-hole stitch in lacking the tiny knot at the head of each stitch needed for strength in hand-worked buttonholes.

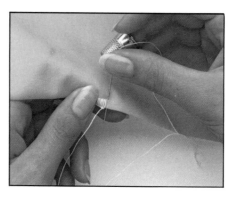

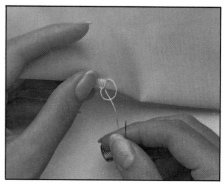

1 Work from left to right with the edge of the fabric and the needle pointing toward you.

2 Pass the thread under the needle for each stitch to form a loop and pull up thread until loop sits on fabric edge.

Bar tack

A bar tack is used to strengthen a weak point in construction—for example, the lower edge of a zipper opening, the end of a slit opening or the seam ends where a pocket is enclosed in a side seam.

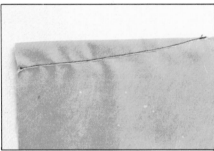

1 Secure thread at back of work and bring through to right side. Work three or four long stitches in the same place, making them the length required for the bar tack.

2 Work closely spaced blanket stitches around the group of straight stitches until they are covered.

Waistline darts

Darts are used to help shape the garment to fit the curves of the body. The rounded fullness they produce should point to the fullest part of the body curve. For example, bust darts should point to the fullest part of the bust; waistline darts in a bodice should also point toward the fullest part of the bust; waistline darts in a skirt or pants should end just above the fullest part of the hip; elbow darts should point toward the tip of the elbow; shoulder darts should point toward the shoulder blades.

Darts should be pressed over a tailor's ham or press mitt to give the correct curve to the garment. Waistline darts and shoulder darts are pressed toward the center front and center back. Bust and elbow darts are pressed downward.

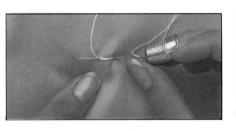

1 With right sides together, matching stitching lines, fold dart down the center and pin, placing the pins on the stitching line at right angles to it. Baste and stitch the dart, beginning at the waistline edge and stitching to the point, taking the last two or three stitches directly on the fold. This prevents a bulge where the dart ends.

2 Fasten thread ends securely by knotting or working a double backstitch by hand.
To press the dart, place it over a tailor's ham or the ironing board with the wrong side up. Press along each side of the stitching, then press the dart toward the center.

Paul Williams

Pants: directions for making (2)

The directions that follow tell you how to complete the basic pants begun on page 59.

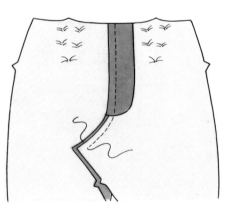

1 Stitch the front crotch seam from the circle to within 1⅜in (3.5cm) of the inside leg seam. Insert the zipper into the center front opening as instructed for a fly-front zipper.

2 Baste the front and back waist darts. Fold each front leg in half vertically, wrong sides together, and run a line of basting down the fold. Repeat on the back leg pieces, starting the line of basting at a point level with the crotch point, so that the crease, when it is pressed in, will begin at the base of the buttocks.

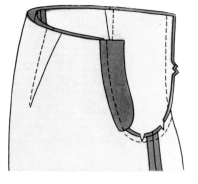

6 Turn one leg inside out and slip it inside the other leg. With right sides together, matching notches and inside leg seams, baste and stitch the remainder of the crotch seam. Clip curves and press the seam open.

7 Press the creases along marked lines, using a damp cloth and pressing firmly.

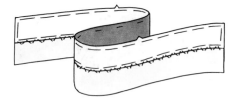

3 With right sides together and notches matching, baste the side seams, the inside leg seams, and the back crotch seam together. Try on the pants and check the fit. Mark any necessary adjustments, distributing the increase or decrease evenly. Check the crease lines (vertical basting) to make sure they hang straight. If they slant towards the inside of the leg, raise the pants at the waistline on the appropriate side until the crease hangs straight. The excess seam allowance at waistline should be trimmed away when the pants are removed.

8 Baste the interfacing to the wrong side of the notched edge of waistband. Catch-stitch interfacing to foldline.

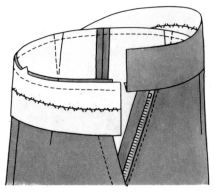

9 With right sides together, matching notches to side seams, baste and stitch the waistband to the waistline of pants. Press seam toward waistband.

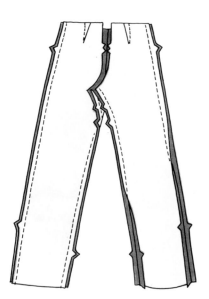

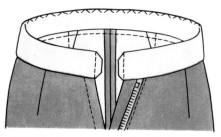

4 Take of the pants and remove the basting from the back crotch seam. Stitch the darts and press them toward the center. Stitch the side seams. Finish seams and press open.

5 Baste and stitch the inside leg seams, easing in fullness between the back notches to fit the front. Finish seams and press open.

10 With right sides together, fold the waistband along the foldline, baste and stitch ends. Trim interfacing close to stitching. Grade seam allowances and cut across corners.

pattern pack

11 Turn waistband right side out and baste close to folded edge. On the inside, turn under the seam allowance of the waistband and hem to stitching line. Press. Sew hook and eye to waistband at center front opening.

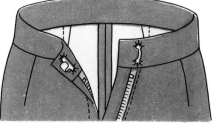

12 Try on the pants and mark the hem. Turn up hem and baste close to folded edge. Trim hem to an even width. Finish the raw edge of hem by turning in $\frac{1}{4}$in (5mm) and machine stitching—or, if the fabric is thick, finish by overcasting. Sew hem to pants, using catch-stitch or hemming stitch.

Terry Evans

Jean-Claude Volpelière

Needlework / COURSE 4

*Appliqué
*Making a template
*Applying an appliqué
*Straight stitch and hand
 application
*Decorating a child's terry
 top

Appliqué

Appliqué provides one of the easiest and fastest ways to decorate almost anything made from fabric, from a child's overalls to delicate table linens. It involves sewing one or more pieces of fabric cut into decorative shapes to a background fabric by hand or machine. Because a wide range of shapes, colors, patterns and textures can be used, appliqué also offers plenty of opportunity for creative design.

Materials

Appliqué is easiest when the fabrics used for both backing and decoration are firmly woven and do not ravel easily. But other fabrics can be used. Non-woven felt works well, for example, and softly woven, easily frayed, stretchable, and delicate fabrics can be backed with iron-on interfacing to make them usable. If the finished article is to be washed, all fabrics used should be pre-shrunk and colorfast.

The type of thread to use depends on the effect you want to achieve. If you want to feature the stitching, use a contrasting color or a contrasting texture such as embroidery cotton or wool. The thread, like the fabric, however, must withstand the wear and the care the finished item will have. For purely functional stitching, use sewing thread in a color that matches either the appliqué or the background fabric.

Making a template

The first step in appliqué is to make a pattern or template for use in cutting out the decorative shapes. Trace all the pieces in the design separately on tracing paper leaving at least $\frac{1}{2}$in (1.3cm) between them. Place the traced design over a piece of cardboard. Slip a sheet of dressmaker's carbon paper between the layers — regular carbon paper would smudge.

Draw around the shapes with a dry ballpoint pen. Remove the design and carbon paper from the cardboard and cut out the shapes. You may use sharp scissors for cutting, but a knife with a razor blade for the cutting edge is easier to control and makes a neat, clean edge around the template.

Simon Butcher

Applying an appliqué with zig-zag or satin stitch

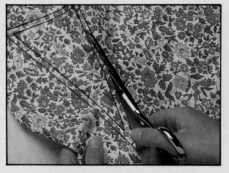

1 Place template right side up on the right side of appliqué material. Hold in place and trace around the edges with a pencil or tailor's chalk. Remove template. Mark out $\frac{1}{4}$in (5mm) from the edges of the outline and draw a second outline $\frac{1}{4}$in (5mm) larger all around than the first. Repeat for other appliqué pieces.

2 Cut out appliqué pieces along the outer outlines.

3 Pin first appliqué piece in position on the background and baste around it along the inner outline.

4 With machine, straight stitch around the appliqué along the basting line. Remove basting.

5 Trim off seam allowance as close to the machine stitching as possible. Add other appliqué pieces in the correct sequence to background using the same procedure.

6 Zig-zag (or satin stitch by hand) over the straight stitching and raw edges of appliqué pieces.

Straight stitch and hand application

1 Trace templates, remove and draw second outline $\frac{1}{4}$in (5mm) larger all around each shape as for zig-zag application above, but do not cut out. Stitch by machine or with tiny hand stitches along the inner outline of each shape. Cut out each shape along the outer outline.

2 Turn seam allowances to the wrong side along the stitched lines. Baste and press. Clip corners and at curves as necessary to eliminate bulk.

3 Pin and baste appliqué pieces in place on the ground fabric and slip stitch around the edges with tiny hand stitches. Remove basting.

Simon Butcher

Fly a kite

Stitch this multi-colored kite to the back of a ready-made beach cover-up or jacket.

Simon Butcher

Materials

Ready-made terrycloth top in child's size
10×15in (25.5×38cm) piece of iron-on interfacing (if terry top is stretchable)
6×9in (15×23cm) rectangles of closely woven cotton in green, yellow, and a coordinating print
Tracing paper
Hard pencil
Dressmaker's carbon paper
Dry ballpoint pen
Thin cardboard
Sharp-pointed scissors
Red sewing thread

To make

1 Trace the kite on page 69 and position the tracing against the back of the garment with top point about $2\frac{1}{2}$in (6.5cm) below the neck seam and slightly to one side. The lower end should be slightly to the other side of the back. Mark the 4 corners of the kite on the garment with light pencil marks, pins, or tailor's tacks.

2 On a new piece of tracing paper, trace as separate pieces each of the 3 triangles in the kite and each bow on the tail. Transfer these shapes to the cardboard using dressmaker's carbon paper.

3 Cut out templates for each shape from the cardboard. Number the templates as shown on page 69 and mark the right side of each.

4 Place templates 3, 4, and 5 on the green fabric alowing at least $\frac{1}{2}$in (1.3cm) between each shape. Draw around each template with a sharp pencil. Remove the templates.

5 Draw another outline around the outside of each shape $\frac{1}{4}$in (5mm) larger all around.

6 Follow the same procedure with template 1 on the print material and 2 on the yellow.

7 Cut out the 5 shapes along the outer outlines.

8 If the garment is stretchable, place the interfacing on the wrong side of the back making sure it covers the whole area where the kite will be located and at least 4in (10cm) below the kite for the tail. Iron the interfacing in place. This will prevent the garment from stretching in the area of the appliqué.

9 Pin the print (No. 1) triangle in place on the garment with its 2 narrow angles just beyond the marks. Baste in position along inner pencil lines. Stitch along basting line and trim off seam allowance as close to the stitching as possible.

10 Pin and baste the yellow (No. 2) triangle in position, making sure the inner pencil line on its second longest side lies directly over the stitched seam of the print triangle. Baste and stitch along inner pencil lines. Trim seam allowance.

11 Set machine for zig-zag stitch. The stitches should be about $\frac{1}{4}$in (5mm) wide and close together. Using red

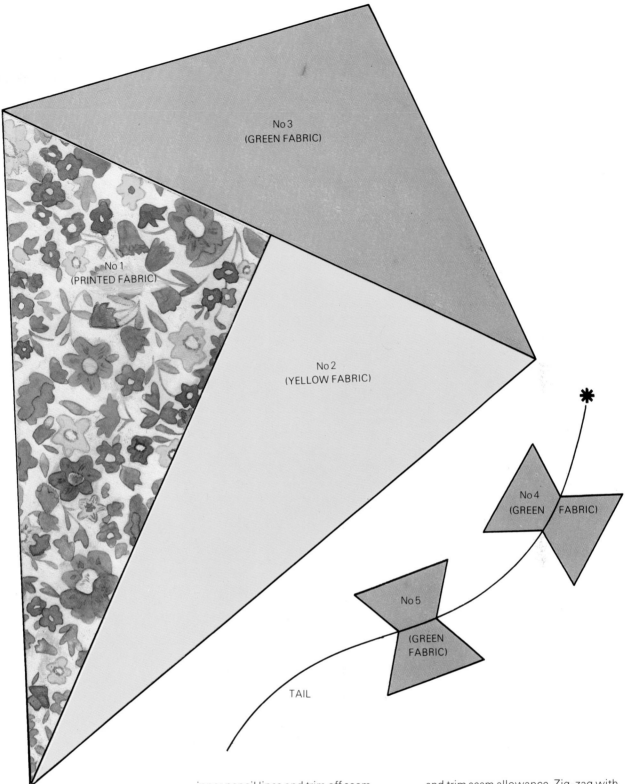

No 3
(GREEN FABRIC)

No 1
(PRINTED FABRIC)

No 2
(YELLOW FABRIC)

No 4
(GREEN   FABRIC)

No 5

(GREEN
FABRIC)

TAIL

John Hutchinson

thread, zig-zag down the outer edges of the kite over the straight stitch seams and the raw edges of the triangles. Then zig-zag over the center seam.
12 Pin and baste the green (No. 3) triangle in position aligning it with the straight stitched seams along the tops of the other 2 triangles. Stitch along the

inner pencil lines and trim off seam allowance.
13 Zig-zag over the stitched seams starting with the seam across the center and then covering the outer edges.
14 Draw the tail on the garment with a pencil or tailor's chalk or baste it in and cover with a narrow zig-zag stitch.
15 Pin bows in position on tail. Baste along inner pencil lines, straight stitch

and trim seam allowance. Zig-zag with narrow stitch.
16 On inside of garment, gently pull away interfacing (if used) outside the area of the appliqué and trim away excess close to stitching.
17 If you do not have a zig-zag machine follow the directions for applying an appliqué by hand and straight stitch on page 67.

EXTRA SPECIAL CROCHET

Popcorn sweaters

Choose either a tweed or solid-color yarn to make this bulky sweater. It is worked in double crochet with bands of popcorn stitch and knitted ribbing.

S. Wells

Size
To fit 26[28:30]in (66[71:76]cm) chest. Length, 13¾[16:19]in (35[41:49]cm). Sleeve seam, 12½[13¾:15]in (32[35:38]cm).
Note: instructions for larger sizes are in brackets; one set of figures applies to all sizes.

Materials
23[25:27]oz (650[700:750]g) of a bulky yarn
Size H (5.5mm) crochet hook
1 pair No. 7 (5mm) knitting needles

Gauge
11dc to 4in (10cm) on Size H (5.5mm) hook.

Front
**Using Size H (5.5mm) hook chain 41[43:35].
Base row 1dc into 4th ch from hook, 1dc into each ch to end, turn.
Next row Ch 3 to count as first dc, now work 1dc into each dc to end, working last dc into top of the 3ch, turn. (39[41:43]dc). begin patt.
1st row (RS) Ch 3, *work 4dc all into next dc, remove hook from loop and insert it into first of the 4dc worked, replace dropped loop on hook and draw through loop of first dc—popcorn formed, 1dc into next dc, rep from * to end of row, turn. (19[20:21] popcorns.)
2nd row Ch 3, 1dc into first popcorn, * work a popcorn into next dc, 1dc into next popcorn, rep from * to within last dc, 1dc into last dc, turn.
3rd row Ch 3, 1dc into next dc, *1dc into next popcorn, 1dc into next dc, rep from * to end, turn. (39[41:43]dc.)
4th-8th rows Ch 3, 1dc into each dc to end, turn. These 8 rows form the patt. ** Cont. in patt, work 6[10:13] rows more.

Shape neck
Patt over first 13[14:15]dc, work next 2dc tog, turn and work on these dc for first side of neck. Work 2dc tog at neck edge on next 1[2:2] rows. Fasten off.
Skip center 9dc for neck, join yarn to next dc, work 2dc tog, then patt to end of row. Complete to match first side.

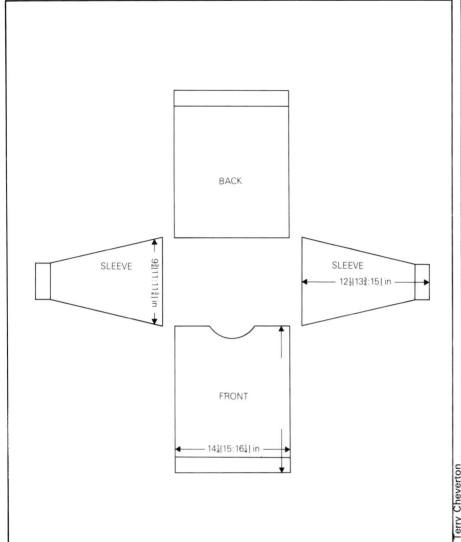

Diagram labels:
- BACK
- SLEEVE — 9¾[11:11¾] in
- SLEEVE — 12½[13¾:15] in
- FRONT — 14¼[15:16¼] in

Terry Cheverton

Technique tip

How to make a popcorn

Popcorn is the name given to the type of bobble used in this pattern. The idea is to work a number of stitches into one stitch and then draw them together, so making the bobble protrude from the background fabric.

This popcorn is made of four double crochet worked into one stitch.

After working the four doubles remove the hook from the loop and insert it into the first of the four doubles.

keeping the hook in the first double, insert it into the dropped loop. Draw this loop through the first double, so gathering the four doubles closely together to form the popcorn.

The popcorns are spaced across the row to prevent the fabric from spreading — as it would if they were placed close together.

Coral Mula

Waistband

With RS facing join yarn and using No. 7 (5mm) needle pick up and K 39[41:43] sts along lower edge.
1st rib row P1, (K1, P1) to end.
2nd rib row K1, (P1, K1) to end.
Rep these 2 rows for 2in (5cm). Bind off loosely in rib.

Back

Work as given for front from ** to **
Continue in patt, work until back is same length as front. Fasten off.
mark the 13th[13th:14th]st from each side edge to denote shoulders.

Waistband

Work as given for front waistband.

Sleeves

Using Size H (5.5mm) hook ch 21[23:25]. Work base row and next row as for front then proceed in patt but inc 1 dc at each end of 3rd and every following fourth row by working 2dc into dc at each end of row, until 27[29:33]dc remain. Fasten off.

Cuff

With RS facing join yarn and using No. 7 (5mm) needles pick up and K 27[29:31] sts evenly along lower edge. Work the 2 rib rows of waistband for 1½in (4cm). Bind off loosely in rib.

Turtleneck

Join right shoulder seam. With RS facing join yarn to top of left front neck and using No. 7 (5mm) needle pick up and K 10[11:12] sts along left front neck. 13 sts across center front neck, 10[11:12] sts along right front neck and 22[24:26] sts across back neck to marker. 55[59:63] sts. Work the 2 rib rows of waistband for 5in (12.5cm); end rib row 1. Bind off in rib.

To finish

Do not block. Join left shoulder and collar seam. Mark depth of armholes 5[5½:6]in (12.5[14:15]cm) from shoulder seams on back and front. Sew the sleeves to the armholes between markers. Join side and sleeve seams. Fold the collar to the right side.

CROCHET

Bobbles and Champagne

"Effervescent" is the word for this glamorous evening sweater worked in a lacy pattern with bobbles. Wear it for your next special occasion and watch the heads turn.

Sizes
To fit 32/34[36/38]in (83/87[92/97]cm) bust.
Length, 23½in (59cm).
Sleeve length, 20in (51cm).

Note Directions for larger size are given in brackets []; where there is only one set of figures it applies to both sizes.

Materials
34[39]oz (950[1050]g) cotton sportweight yarn
Size C (3mm) crochet hook

Gauge
1 patt rep (12 sts) and 6 rows to 2¼in (6mm) on size C (3mm) hook.

Back
With size C (3mm) hook ch 113[125].
Base row 1dc into 4th ch from hook, 1dc into each ch to end. Turn.
1st patt row (RS) 3ch to count as first dc, 1dc into each of next 3sts, work 5dc all into next st, remove hook from loop and insert if from *front to back* into first of the 5dc worked, replace dropped loop on hook and draw through loop of first dc—called front bobble (FB); now work *1dc into each of next 11 sts, FB into next dc, rep from * to within last 10 sts, 1dc into each of last 10 sts. Turn. 9[10] FB.
2nd patt row 3ch, *1dc into each of next 7dc, work 5dc all into next st, remove hook from loop and insert it from *back to front* into first of the 5dc worked, replaced dropped loop on hook and draw through loop of first dc—called back bobble (BB); 1dc into next dc, 1dc into top of next bobble, 1dc into next dc, BB into next dc, rep from * to within last 2dc, 1dc into each of last 2dc. Turn. 18[20] BB.
3rd patt row As first patt row.
4th patt row 4ch to count as 1dc and 1ch, skip next dc, 1dc into next dc, *1ch, skip next dc, BB into next dc, (1ch, skip next st, 1dc into next dc) twice, 1ch, skip next dc, 1dc into top of next bobble, (1ch, skip next dc, 1dc into next dc) twice, rep from * to end. Turn. 9[10] BB.
5th patt row 4ch, 1dc into next dc, (1ch, 1dc into next dc) twice, 1ch, FB into next dc, 1ch, 1dc into top of next bobble, 1ch, FB into next dc, *(1ch, 1dc into next dc) 3 times, FB into next dc, 1ch, 1dc into top of next bobble, 1ch, FB into next dc, rep from * to within last sp, 1ch, 1dc into last dc. Turn. 18[20] FB.
6th patt row 4ch, 1dc into top of next

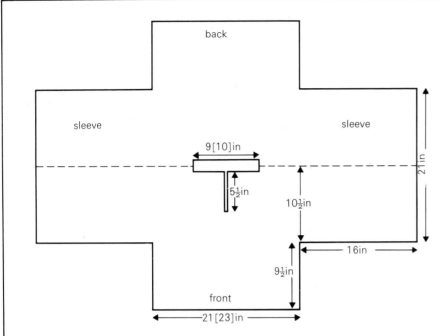

Diagram labels: back, sleeve, sleeve, front, 9[10]in, 5½in, 10½in, 21in, 16in, 9½in, 21[23]in

bobble, *1ch, BB into next dc, 1ch, 1dc into top of next bobble, (1ch, 1dc into next dc) 3 times, 1ch, 1dc into top of next bobble, rep from * to end, but work last dc into 3rd of the 4ch. Turn.

7th patt row 3ch, 1dc into first sp, 1dc into next dc, 1dc into next sp, *FB into next dc, (1dc into next sp, 1dc into next st) 5 times, 1dc into next sp, rep from * to end, working last dc into 3rd of the 4ch. Turn.

8th patt row As 2nd patt row.

9th patt row As first patt row.
rows 4 to 9 form the patt. Rep them twice more, then work rows 4 to 6 again. Using a separate ball of yarn work 84ch for 2nd sleeve and leave aside.

Next row Work 86ch for first sleeve, 1dc into 4th ch from hook, 1dc into each of next 2ch, *FB into next ch, 1dc into each of next 11ch*, rep from * to * to within last 8ch, FB into next ch, 1dc into each of last 7ch, patt across back, then work across ch of second sleeve working 1dc into first ch; rep from * to * to within last 10ch, 1dc into each of last 10ch, turn. 23[24] FB. Cont in patt until the 8th patt from beg has been completed. Fasten off.

Waistband
Using size C (3mm) hook ch22.
Base row 1sc into 3rd ch from hook, 1sc into each ch to end. Turn. 20sc.
Patt row 2ch to count as first sc, working into back loop only work 1sc into each sc to end. Turn.
Rep the patt row 78[84] times more. Do not turn but work 1sc into each row end along edge. Fasten off

Front
Work as given for back until 6th row of 5th patt from beg has been worked.

Divide for opening
Next row Work across first 69[72]sps, turn and work on first set of sps until 7th patt from beg has been completed.

Shape neck
Next row Work to within last 22[24]sts, turn. Cont in patt until front is same length as back. Fasten off. With RS facing skip center sp, join yarn to next dc and work as given for first side reversing shaping at neck.

Waistband
Work as given for back waistband.

Cuffs (make 2)
Work as for waistband but rep the patt row 39 times in all.

To finish
With RS facing join yarn to lower edge of back and work 80[86]sc evenly along edge, turn. With waistband at back of work and working through the double thickness, work 1sc into each sc to end, so joining waistband to back. Fasten off. Join waistband to edge of front in the same way.
Join upper sleeve and shoulder seams. With RS facing join yarn to sleeve edge and work 1sc into each row end along this edge, turn. Join cuff to lower edge of sleeve as for back waistband but decrease 14sc evenly across the sleeve edge. Fasten off. Join other cuff in the same way. Join side and sleeve seams.

Neck edging
With RS facing join yarn to base of opening and work 1sc into each row end along right side of opening to neck, 4ch, skip next 2sts, *1dc into next st,

1ch, skip next st, rep from * all around neck, then work 1sc into each row end along left side of opening, turn.
Next row 1ch, work 1sc into each sc and 1sc into each dc and sp all around neck and opening. Fasten off.

Neck tie
Using yarn double work a length of ch approximately 61 in (156cm). Fasten off.

Tie trims (make 2)
Using yarn single 4ch, sl st into first ch to form a circle.
Next round 3ch, 15dc into circle, sl st into top of the 3ch. Fasten off.
Thread tie through holes at neck, then attach a tie trim to each end.

Technique tip
Working into one loop only

When you work a basic stitch, such as single, half double or double crochet, you will see that a chain is formed at the top of the stitch.

Usually the stitches on the following row are worked into both loops of the chain, but you can, instead, work a stitch into either the front or back loop only.

When you do this, you produce a different effect: the remaining loops on the previous row make a ridge on the fabric.

This ridged effect is not only decorative but also useful for waistbands and cuffs—as on our evening sweater—for it serves as a kind of mock ribbing.

Coral Mula

Flower shawl

A delicate border of blossoms and lace trims this lovely shawl for a baby, made in a fine random pastel yarn. The main part of the shawl is worked in doubles accented with swirling lines of openwork.

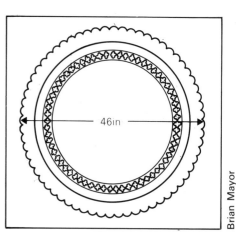

Brian Mayor

Size
46in [117cm] diameter when pressed.

Materials
10oz [260g] of a 3 ply sport weight yarn
Size C (3.00mm) crochet hook

Gauge
26dc to 4in (10cm).

To make
Work 4ch and sl st into first ch to form a circle.
1st round (5ch, 1sc into circle) 8 times, sl st into center of first loop. 8 loops.
2nd round 1sc into first loop, (4ch, 1sc into next loop) 7 times, 4ch, 1dc into first sc.
3rd round 2dc into first loop, (3ch, 1dc into next sc, 2dc into next loop) 7 times.
4th round (3ch, skip next dc, 1dc into each of next 2 sts, 2dc into next loop) 8 times.
5th round (3ch, skip next dc, 1dc into each of next 3 sts, 2dc into next loop) 8 times.
6th round (3ch, skip next dc, 1dc into each of next 4 sts, 2dc into next loop) 8 times.
7th round (3ch, skip next dc, 1dc into each of next 5 sts, 2dc into next loop) 8 times.
8th round (3ch, skip next dc, 1dc into each of next 6 sts, 2dc into next loop) 8 times.
Work 3 more rounds working 1 more dc between the 2dc worked into each loop.

S. Wells

11dc in each panel.

12th round (3ch, skip next dc, 1dc into each of next 5 sts, 3ch, skip next 2 sts, 1dc into each of next 3 sts, 2dc into next loop) 8 times.

13th round (3ch, skip next dc, 1dc into each of next 4 sts, 2dc into next loop) 16 times.

14th round (3ch, skip next dc, 1dc into each of next 5 sts, 2dc into next loop) 16 times.

15th round (3ch, skip next dc, 1dc into each of next 6 sts, 2dc into next loop) 16 times.

Work 5 rounds, working 1 more dc between the 2dc worked into each loop. 13dc in each panel.

21st round (3ch, skip next dc, leaving last loop of each on hook work 1dc into each of next 2dc, yo and draw a loop through all 3 loops on hook – 1dc decreased, 1dc into each of next 10dc, 2dc into next loop) 16 times.

22nd round (3ch, 1dc into each of next 12dc, 2dc into next loop) 16 times.

23rd round (3ch, 1dc into each of next 13dc, 2dc into next loop) 16 times.

24th round (3ch, 1dc into each of next 14dc, 2dc into next loop) 16 times.

Dec in this way on next and foll 4th round and then work 3 rounds without shaping. 32 rounds worked, 22dc in each panel.

Cont in patt, dec 1dc at beg of every panel on next and every 3rd round until 55 rounds from beg have been worked, ending with 3ch, sl st into first st of next panel. 37dc in each panel.

56th round 3ch, 1dc into each of next 36 sts, 3dc into next loop (1dc into each of next 37 sts, 3dc into next loop) 15 times, sl st into top of the 3ch.

Start flower insertion:

57th round 11ch, 1tr into same place as sl st, *4ch, skip next 4 sts, 1sc into next st, 4ch, skip next 4 sts, now work 1tr, 4ch, 1 triple triple (tr tr), 4ch, and 1tr all into next st, rep from * to last 9 sts, 4ch, skip next 4 sts, 1sc into next st, 4ch, skip next 4 sts, 1tr into base of 11ch, 4ch, sl st into 7th of the 11ch.

58th round *4ch, leaving last loop of each on hook work 4dtr all into next tr so having 5 loops on hook, yo and draw through 4 loops on hook – petal formed, work a petal into next sc and a petal into next tr; now leaving last loop of each on hook work 3dtr all into next tr tr, yo and draw through first 3 loops on hook – half petal formed, yo and draw through all 5 loops on hook, 5ch, sl st into top of same tr tr that half petal was worked into, rep from * to end, finishing sl st into base of 4ch at beg of round.

59th round *Work a half petal into center of next petal group but draw through 4 loops on hook, (4ch, 1 petal into center of same group but draw through 5 loops on hook) 3 times, 4ch,

sl st into next sl st of previous round, rep from * to end.

60th round 7ch, 1tr into top of next petal, *6ch, 1sc into top of next petal, 6ch, leaving last loop of each on hook work 1tr into next petal, 1tr tr into next sl st, 1tr into top of next petal, yo and draw through all 4 loops on hook, rep from * to end, finishing with a tr into top of last petal, sl st into top of 7ch.

61st round 3ch, 5dc into next 6-ch sp, *1dc into next sc, 5dc into next 6-ch sp, rep from * to end, finishing with 5dc all into last 6-ch sp, sl st into top of the 3ch.

62nd round 3ch, *1dc into next st, (1ch, skip next st, 1dc into next st) twice, 1dc into next st, rep from * to last 4 sts, 1dc into next st, (1ch, skip next st, 1dc into next st) twice, sl st into top of the 3ch.

63rd round 3ch, *1dc into next sp, 2dc into next dc, 1dc into next sp, 1dc into each of next 3dc, rep from * to last 5 sts, 1dc into next sp, 2dc into next dc, 1dc into next sp, 1dc into last 2dc, sl st into top of the 3ch.

64th round 5ch, (1tr into same place as sl st, 1ch) 4 times, 1tr into same st, *skip next 2 sts, 1sc into next st, 4ch, skip next 3 sts, 1tr into next st, 4ch, skip next 3 sts, 1sc into next st, skip next 2 sts, 1tr into next st, (1ch, 1tr into same st) 5 times, rep from * to last 11 sts, skip next 2 sts, 1sc into next st, 4ch, skip next 3 sts, 1tr into next st, 4ch, skip next 3 sts, 1sc into next st, sl st into 4th of the 5ch.

65th round Sl st to center of first 6-tr group, *4ch, 1tr into next single tr, (1ch and 1tr) 5 times into same single tr, 4ch, 1sc between 3rd and 4th tr of next 6-tr group, rep from * to end, sl st into sl st at beg of round.

66th round *(5ch, leaving last loop of each on hook work 1tr into each of next 2 sts, yo and draw through all 3 loops on hook – V formed) 3 times, 5ch, 1sc into next sc, rep from * to end, sl st into base of 5ch at beg of round.

67th round Sl st to top of first V, 9ch, *1tr into same st, work 1tr, 5ch, 1tr, 5ch and 1tr all into next V, 1tr, 5ch and 1tr all into next V, rep from * to within last 2 Vs, 1tr, 5ch, 1tr, 5ch and 1tr all into next V, 1tr, 5ch and 1tr into next V, sl st into 4th ch at beg of round.

68th round *3ch, 1sc into same st, 7ch, skip next tr, 1sc into next tr, 3ch, 1sc into same st, 7ch, 1sc into next tr, 3ch, 1sc into same st, 7ch, skip next tr, 1sc into next tr, 3ch, 1sc into same st, 7ch, 1sc into next tr, rep from * to end, sl st into base of the 3ch. Fasten off.

Press shawl lightly on the wrong side, using a cool iron over a dry cloth.

Technique tip

Forming the flowers

The stitches at the top of the petals are drawn together to give a good shape. To do this you need to leave the last loop of each stitch worked on the hook, to be drawn through at a later stage.

To complete the top of the petal, place yarn over hook and draw it through 4 of the loops on the hook. You will now have 2 loops on the hook. After working each petal you will have an extra loop on the hook.

When four petals have been worked you will have 5 loops on the hook. Place yarn over hook and draw through these 5 loops, so drawing the centers of the petals together. The first half of the flower has been formed.

Continue to work around the shawl and finish the round as instructed in the pattern. To form the second half of the flower you work 4 petals into the center of the first half of the flower. You now have 8 petals in each complete flower.

CROCHET

Anti-freeze

This zip-up jacket is just the thing for those cold days. It is made in a bulky yarn using a simple stitch which produces a ridged effect.

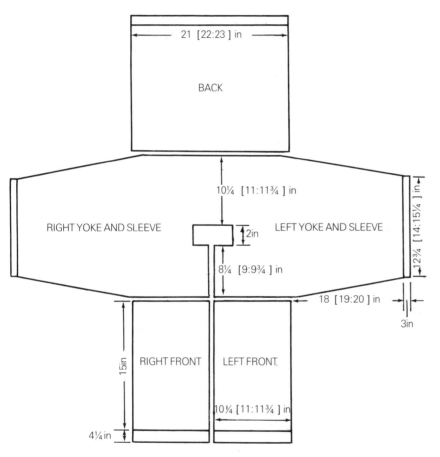

John Hutchinson

Sizes
To fit, 38[40:42]in (97[102:107]cm) chest.
Length, 29½[30¼:31]in (75[76.5:78.5]cm).
Sleeve seam, 21[22:23]in (53[56:58.5]cm).

Note Directions for larger sizes are in brackets []; where there is only one set of figures it applies to all sizes.

Materials
48[50:52]oz (1350[1400:1450]g) of a bulky knitting yarn
Sizes H and K (5.00 and 7.00mm) crochet hooks
1 × 23½in (60cm) open-ended zipper

Gauge
12 sts and 10 rows to 4in (10cm) in patt st on size K (7.00mm) hook.

Back
using size K (7.00mm) hook chain 64[67:70].
Base row 1sc into 2nd ch from hook, 1sc into each sc to end. Turn. (63[66:69]sc.)
Patt row (RS) 1ch, working into the back loop only, work 1sc into each sc to end. Turn.
Rep the patt row until work measures 15in (38cm) from bag. Fasten off.

Left front
Using size K (7.00mm) hook chain 32[34:36].

Base row 1sc into 2nd ch from hook, 1sc into each ch to end. Turn. 31[33:35]sc.
Patt row (RS) 1ch, working into the back loop, work 1sc into each sc to end. Turn. Rep the patt row until work measures 15in (38cm) from beg. Fasten off.

Right front
Work as given for left front.

Right yoke and sleeve
Using size K (7.00mm) hook chain 32[34: 36] for back yoke. Work base row and patt row as for back. 31[33:35]sc. Cont in patt until work measures 4[4:4¼]in (10[10:10.5]cm) from beg, ending at neck edge. Fasten off.
Using size K (7.00mm) hook chain 26[28:30] for right front yoke. Work base row and patt row as for back, then cont in patt until work is 1 row longer than back yoke, so ending at neck edge. Do not turn work but make 6ch, then patt across back yoke. 62[66:70]sc. Cont in patt on these 62[66:70]sc until yoke fits along top edge of front; mark ends of last row.
Shape for sleeve
Dec 1sc at each end of next row by working 2sc together.
Work 3 rows straight.
Rep last 4 rows 11 times more.
38[42:46]sts rem. Cont without shaping until sleeve measures 18[19:20]in (45.5[48.5:51]cm). Fasten off.

Left yoke and sleeve
Using size K (7.00mm) hook chain 26[28:30] for left front yoke. Work base row as for back then cont in patt for 4in (10cm). Fasten off. Using size K (7.00mm) hook chain 32[34:36] for back yoke. Work base row and patt row as for back, then cont in patt until work is 1 row longer than front, so ending at neck edge. Do not turn work but make 6ch, then patt across front yoke. Cont in patt on these 62[66:70]sc to match right yoke and sleeve.

To finish
With WS of back yokes together and working through double thickness work 1sc into each sc to end (seam edge will be on RS). Working sc on the RS of work join back and fronts to lower edge of yoke, between markers, then join side and sleeve seams in the same way.

Cuffs (alike)
Using size H (5.00mm) hook chain 6, 1sc into 2nd ch from hook, 1sc into each ch to end. Turn.
Next row 1ch, working into the back loop only, inc as foll: work 1sc into first sc, 1sc into each sc to within last sc, 2sc into last sc. Turn. (7sc). Rep last row once more. 9sc. Cont in patt, without shaping, work 28[30:32] rows. Do not turn work but work 28[30:32]sc along the long edge, omitting shaped section.

S. Wells

77

Fasten off.
Join cuff to sleeve by working 28[30:32] sc along lower edge of sleeve, then with WS facing join cuff to sleeve with sc, so that seam is on WS of work.

Collar
Using size K (7.00mm) hook and with WS facing work 36[39:41]sc around neck edge, turn, work in patt for 7 rows.
Next row Work to end increasing 12sc evenly across this row. 47[50:52]sc. Cont without shaping, work 8 rows. Fasten off.

Waistband
Using size H (5.00mm) hook chain 14.
Base row 1 sc into 2nd ch from hook, 1sc into each ch to end. Turn.
Cont in patt as for back. Work 98[102: 106] rows. Dec 1sc at each end of next 4 rows by working 2sc tog. 5sc. Fasten off. With RS facing join yarn to top right-hand corner and working along long edge work 98[102:106]sc, omitting shaped section at end. Fasten off. Join waistband to jacket on WS of work as for cuffs.

Edging
Using size H (5.00mm) hook work a row of sc very firmly along edge of each front. Sew in zipper and press lightly

Technique tip

Joining the back yoke

The back yoke is worked in two pieces and should be joined so that the seam is not obvious. To do this work the seam on the right side of the fabric, forming a ridge which will blend in with the pattern of the jacket.
Place the wrong sides of both pieces together with the edges to be joined level. Insert the crochet hook into the first loop at right-hand edge of both pieces. Wind yarn around hook and draw a loop through, then work 1 chain.

and work 1 single crochet to join the pieces.

Continue in this way all along the row. Fasten off. When the yoke is laid flat the seam blends with the pattern.

Insert hook into next loop on first piece and corresponding loop on second piece

Coral Mula

CROCHET

A cardigan with class

Jean-Claude Volpeliere

This glamorous crocheted cardigan with knitted ribbing teams up beautifully with a simple long skirt or dress. Made in a silky yarn, it is perfect for casual or dressier cool evenings.

Sizes
To fit 34[36:38]in (87[92:97]cm) bust.
Length, $24\frac{1}{2}$[$24\frac{3}{4}$:$25\frac{1}{4}$]in (62[63:64]cm)
Sleeve seam, $18\frac{1}{2}$in (47cm).

Note Directions for larger sizes are in brackets []; where there is only one set of figures it applies to all sizes.

Materials
19[20:22]oz (26[28:30]g) of 3-ply rayon twist thread
Size C (3.00mm) crochet hook
1 pair No. 1 ($2\frac{1}{2}$mm) knitting needles
6 buttons

Gauge
24 sts and 20 rows to 4in (10cm) in patt worked on size C (3.00mm) hook.

Back
Using size C (3.00mm) hook make 117[123:127]ch.
Base row 1sc into 3rd ch from hook, *1dc into next ch, 1sc into next ch, rep from * to last ch, 1sc into last ch. Turn.
Begin patt.
1st row 3ch, skip first sc, *1sc into next dc, 1dc into next sc, rep from * to last sc, 1dc into last sc. Turn.
2nd row 1ch, sc into first dc, *1dc into next sc, 1sc into next dc, rep from * to end of row, working last sc into top of 3 turning chains. Turn 115[121:125] sts.
These 2 rows form patt. Cont in patt until work measures 19[$19\frac{1}{4}$:$19\frac{3}{4}$]in (48 [49:50]cm) from beg, ending with WS row.
Shape shoulders
Next row Sl st across first 13[13:14] sts. Patt to last 13[13:14] sts. Turn.
Rep last row once more.
Next row Sl st across first 13[15:13] sts, patt to last 13[15:13] sts and leave these unworked, fasten off.
Waistband Using No. 1 ($2\frac{1}{2}$mm) needles and with RS of work facing, pick up and knit 138[144:148] sts along lower edge. Work 50 rows K1, P1 ribbing. Bind off in ribbing.

Left front
Using size C (3.00mm) hook make 53[56: 58]ch. Work base row and patt rows as for back. Cont in patt until work measures 7in (18cm), ending with 2nd patt row.

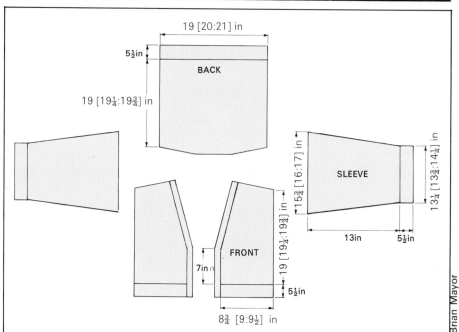

19 [20:21] in

$5\frac{1}{2}$in

BACK

19 [$19\frac{1}{4}$:$19\frac{3}{4}$] in

$15\frac{3}{4}$ [16:17] in

SLEEVE

$13\frac{1}{4}$ [$13\frac{3}{4}$:$14\frac{1}{4}$] in

13in

$5\frac{1}{2}$in

19 [$19\frac{1}{4}$:$19\frac{3}{4}$] in

7in

FRONT

$5\frac{1}{2}$in

$8\frac{3}{4}$ [9:$9\frac{1}{2}$] in

Shape front edge
Keeping patt correct, dec one st at beg on next and every foll 4th row until 39[41:42] sts rem. Continue without shaping until front measures same as back to shoulder, ending at armhole edge.

Shape shoulder
Sl st across first 13[13:14] sts on next row and across first 13[15:13] sts on foll row. Fasten off.

Waistband
Using No. 1 (2½mm) needles and with RS of work facing pick up 68[72:76] sts evenly along lower edge. Work 50 rows K1, P1 rib. Bind off in ribbing.

Right front
Work as given for left front until work measures 7in (18cm), ending with a 1st patt row. Complete as for left front.

Waistband
Work as given for left front waistband

Sleeves
Using size C (3mm) hook ch 83[85:87]. Work the base row as given for back. Continue in patt as for back, inc one st at each end of every 8th row until there are 95[99:103] sts. Continue without shaping until sleeve measures 13in (33cm) from beg. Fasten off.

Cuff
Using No. 1 (2½mm) needles and with RS of work facing pick up 80[82:84] sts along lower edge. Work 50 rows K1, P1 rib. Bind off in ribbing.

Front band
Join shoulder seams. Using No. 1 (2½mm) needles cast on 18sts. Work 4 rows ribbing as given for back.

Next row (buttonhole row) Rib 7, bind off 4 sts, rib to end.
Work the next row in ribbing, casting on 4 sts above those bound off on previous row. Continue working in ribbing, working another buttonhole on every foll 23rd and 24th rows until 6 buttonholes have been made in all. Continue in ribbing, omitting buttonholes, until band is long enough to fit up left front, around neck and down right front when slightly stretched.

To finish
Mark depth of armholes 8¼[8¾:9]in (21[22:23]cm) from shoulder seams on back and fronts and sew sleeves to armholes between markers. Join side and sleeve seams. Sew front band into place up left front, around neck and down right front, easing it to fit.
Sew on buttons.

Technique tip

How to pick up stitches

Picking up stitches on the edge of the fabric to work a waistband or front edging is often more practical than working separate bands, which must then be sewn on to the garment.

The waistband—usually it is in ribbing—is worked downward so that the bound-off edge forms the bottom of the garment or sleeve: there is no difference in the appearance of the ribbing when it is knitted in this way.

It's a good idea to begin by dividing the edge you are working on into sections; this helps you to pick up the stitches evenly across the garment. Fold the work in half and place a pin on the center fold, then divide each side in half again in the same way. Thus, if you are going to pick up 100 stitches altogether, you will know that you must pick up 25 stitches in each section. Hold the work with the right side facing and insert the needle into the edge of the fabric. Loop the yarn around the needle and draw it through for the first stitch. Make sure that the yarn is held to the left, so that it will be at the right end of the needle when you turn and begin knitting. Continue along the edge, drawing a loop through in the same way for each stitch. You can then turn and begin knitting into these loops in the normal way for the edging.

When picking up stitches from worked stitches, insert the needle into the remaining loop of the stitch; when picking up stitches from the row ends, insert the needle into the loop at the end of the row.

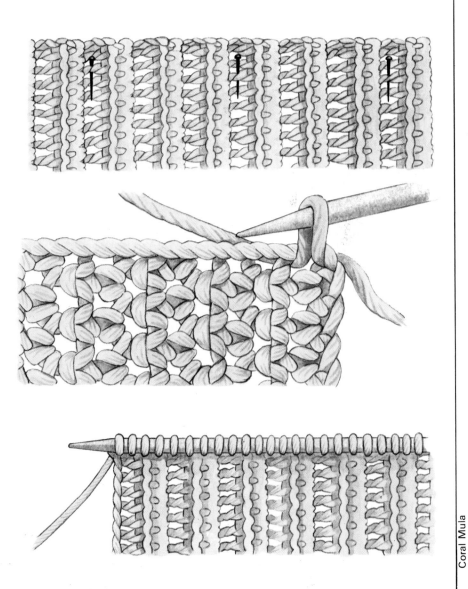

Coral Mula

KNITTING

Make a Fair Isle V-neck vest!

More experienced knitters will enjoy working a traditional Fair Isle pattern. This V-neck would make a really special gift for any man — from sixteen to sixty.

Caroline Arber

Sizes
These directions are for a garment measuring 34½[38:41:44]in (88[97:104:112]cm) around the chest and with a finished back length of 21½[22:22½:23]in (55[56:57:58]cm). Measure the man's chest and decide which size is best.
Note Directions for the larger sizes are in brackets []; where there is only one set of figures it applies to all sizes.

Materials
- 4[4:5:5]oz (100[100:125:125]g) of a sport yarn in color A (medium brown)
- 2[2:3:3]oz (50[50:75:75]g) of colors B (natural) and C (dark brown) and 1oz (25g) each of colors D (gold), E (scarlet), F (coral), G (rust)
- A pair of No. 3 (3¼mm) knitting needles
- No. 2 (2¾mm) and No. 3 (3¼mm) circular needles
- Set of four No. 2 (2¾mm) double-pointed knitting needles

Gauge
15 sts and 16 rows to 2in (5cm) in patt.

Back and front
Using No. 2 (2¾mm) circular needle and A, cast on 240[264:288:312] sts.
Work in round of K1, P1 rib for 4in (10cm), inc 24 sts evenly in last round: 264[288:312:336] sts.
Change to No. 3 (3¼mm) circular needle. Proceed in rounds of stockinette st, working in patt from chart, until work measures 12½in (32cm).

Divide for armholes
Next round Bind off 10, K until there are 113[125:137:149] sts on right-hand (RH) needle, bind off 19, K to last 9 sts, bind off last 9 sts. Cut off yarn.
With wrong side of work facing rejoin yarn to last set of sts and using the pair of No. 3 (3¼mm) needles proceed for back:
Next row Patt to end. Continuing in patt bind off 3 sts at beg of next 4 rows, then 2 sts at beg of following 2[2:4:4] rows. Dec 1 st each end of next and every other row to 91[99:107:115] sts. Work straight until armholes measure 9[9½:9¾:10¼]in (23[24:25:26]cm) from beg, ending with a wrong-side row.

Shape shoulders
Bind off 6[7:7:8] sts at beg of next 6 rows, then 5[5:8:8] sts at beg of next 2 rows. Cut off yarn and place remaining 45[47:49:51] sts on a holder.
With wrong side of work facing join yarn to sts on circular needle and using the pair of No. 3 (3¼mm) needles work front:
Next row Patt 56[62:68:74], turn and

Technique tip

Carrying yarn

This is the way to control two colors in a row of knitting when you are working with blocks of not more than four stitches of any one color. The yarn color not in use is carried in loose strands across the back of the work behind the contrasting stitches until it is needed again.

Be careful not to pull the color not in use too tightly on the wrong side of the work—this is the most common mistake. Since only two colors are used per row, it is possible to control one with each hand. Look at your chart before you begin each row and decide which color predominates; if you are right-handed, you will probably prefer to use this hand to control the most often-used color.

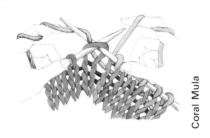

Coral Mula

When the right-hand color is being used, the left hand holds the other color out of the way, below and to the left of the stitches being knitted.

When the left-hand color is being used, the right hand holds the other color out of the way above and to the right of the stitches being knitted.

These diagrams show yarn carried at the back of the work on a knit row—all you will need while you are knitting in rounds, as far as the division for the armhole. From then on, you will be working back and forth in rows, so adapt the same technique for purling stitches.

---

place remaining 57[63:69:75] sts on an extra needle. Work on first set of sts as follows: Patt 1 row. *Bind off 3 sts at side edge twice, then 2 sts at same edge 1 [1:2:2] times, then dec 1 st at same edge 3[5:5:7] times **at the same time** dec 1 st at neck edge on next and every 4th row 2[3:4:5] times, 42[45:48:51] sts. Keeping armhole edge straight continue to dec 1 st at neck on 1st[1st:3rd:3rd] and every 3rd row until 23[26:29:32] sts remain. Work straight until armhole is same depth as back armhole up to beg of shoulder shaping. End at armhole edge.

Shape shoulder

Bind off 6[7:7:8] sts at beg of next row and at same edge twice more. Work 1 row. Bind off. *Return to sts on extra needle. With wrong side facing place next st on a safety pin, join to next st and patt to end. Now work as first side from * to *

Neckband

Join shoulder seams. With right side of work facing join A and using three of the set of four double-pinted needles K back neck sts from holder. Pick up 78[82:86:90] sts along left front neck, K center st from safety pin, then pick up 78[82:86:90] sts along right front neck; 202[212:222:232] sts.
Next round Using 4th needle work in K1, P1 rib to within 2 sts of center front st, P2 tog, K1, P2 tog through back of loops, rib to end. Rep last round for 1 in (2.5cm). Bind off in ribbing, dec as before.

Armbands (alike)

With right side facing join A and using three of the set of four double-pointed needles pick up 140[146:152:158] sts around armhole. Using 4th needle to knit, work in rounds of K1, P1 ribbing for 1 in (2.5cm). Bind off loosely in ribbing.

Technique tips

How to read the chart

● A chart is the easiest way to give directions for a multi-colored pattern. This chart follows the usual practice of each square representing one stitch and each horizontal row of squares representing a row of knitting.

● Always begin at the bottom right-hand square with a knit row and work across the chart to the left, using the background color for any blank square and the appropriate contrast color for any squares that contain a symbol.

● When working back and forth using a pair of needles, work the second row in purl from left to right. Continue in this way up the chart, working odd rows in knit from right to left, and even rows in purl from left to right.

● When working in rounds using a set of four needles or a circular needle, begin every row at the right-hand edge of the chart, and knit every stitch. Use a marker loop of contrasting yarn to remind you where each round begins.

● The individual segments of Fair Isle patterns are called pattern repeats; you work the repeats in succession right across your fabric. The design shown here has a repeat of 12 stitches. When knitting in rounds, the total number of stitches usually corresponds exactly to a multiple of the pattern repeat. When you knit in rows each row has an extra edge stitch (seen on left of chart) to give the fabric a neat edge and complete the motif.

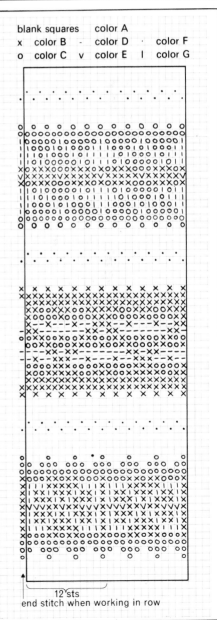

blank squares		color A		
x	color B	-	color D	· color F
o	color C	v	color E	I color G

12 sts
end stitch when working in row

Del Tolton

Loose-look sweater

Gary Warren

A touch of mohair gives extra softness to this comfortable pullover. Made in garter stitch, it's trimmed with panels of cable which you knit separately and sew on.

Sizes
To fit 32[34:36]in (83[87:92]cm) bust.
Length 27¾in (70cm).
Sleeve seam, 15¾in (40cm).
Note Directions for the larger sizes are in brackets []; where there is only one set of figures it applies to all sizes.

Materials
16[18:20]oz (450[500:550]g) of a mohair-type knitting worsted
1 pair No. 9 (6mm) knitting needles
No. 9 (6mm) circular needle
Cable needle

Gauge
13 sts and 26 rows to 4in (10cm) in garter st on No. 9 (6mm) needles.

Front
Using No. 9 (6mm) needles cast on 72 sts and work from side edge to side edge. Cont in garter st until work measures 6¼[6¾:7⅛]in (16[17:18]cm) from beg.
Shape neck
Bind off 3 sts at beg of next and every other row 10 times, ending at neck edge. 42 sts. Cast on 3 sts at beg of next and every other row 10 times. 72 sts. Cont in garter st until work measures 18[19:19¾]in (46[48:50]cm) from beg. Bind off.
Back
Using No. 9 (6mm) needles cast on 72 sts and work from side edge to side edge. Cont in garter st until back measures same as front. Bind off. Join shoulder seams.
Cable panels
Left side Using No. 9 (6mm) needles cast on 10 sts.
1st row (RS) P2, K6, P2.
2nd row K2, P6, K2.
3rd-4th rows As 1st-2nd.
5th row P2, sl next 3 sts onto cable needle and leave at front of work, K3, then K3 sts from cable needle—called C6f—, P2.
6th row As 2nd.
7th-8th rows As 1st-2nd.
These 8 rows form patt. Rep them until strip fits from lower edge of front to shoulder and down to lower edge of back, ending with an 8th patt row. Bind off.
Right side Work in same way as left side, reversing position of cable as follows:
5th row P2, sl 3 sts onto cable needle and leave at back of work, K3, then K3 sts from cable needle—called C6B—, P2.

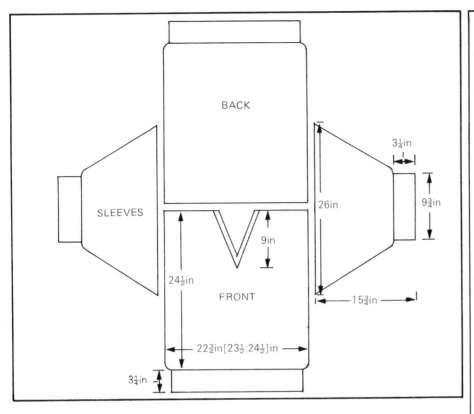

Sew panels in position along side edges of front and back.

Sleeves

Using No. 9 (6mm) needles cast on 31 sts.

1st row (RS) K1, *P1, K1, rep from * to end.

2nd row P1, *K1, P1, rep from * to end. Rep these two rows for 3in (8cm), ending with a 2nd row. Cont in garter st, inc one st at each end of every 3rd row until there are 79 sts. Cont without shaping until sleeve measures 15¾in (40cm) from beg, ending with a WS row. Bind off.

To finish

Do not press. Mark position for sleeves 13in (33cm) down from shoulders on back and front. Sew sleeve top in position. Join side and sleeve seams.

Lower border Using No. 9 (6mm) circular needle and with RS of work facing, pick up and knit one st from each garter st ridge and 16 sts along cable panels at sides—the total number of sts should be even. Work 3in (7.5cm) in rounds of K1, P1 ribbing. Bind off loosely in ribbing.

Neckband Using No. 9 (6mm) circular needle and with RS of work facing, beg at left shoulder and pick up and knit 40 sts down left front neck, one st at center of V (mark this with a loop of colored thread), 40 sts up right front neck and 25 sts across back neck. 106 sts.

Next round (K1, P1) to within 3 sts of marked center st, P3 tog, K center st, P3 tog through back loop, (K1, P1) to end. Rep last round 5 times more. Bind off in rib, dec as before at each side of center.

Technique tip
Working a cable panel

Cable patterns are often used to add textural interest to a garment. On this sweater a simple cable pattern is worked separately and sewed to the side edges of the back and front. Two stitches in reverse stockinette stitch at each side of the cable emphasize its shape and texture. To work a panel of cable that crosses from right to left: On the row on which the cable is to be crossed, purl the first two stitches, and then slip the next three stitches onto a cable needle and leave them at the front of the work.

Knit the next three stitches, then knit the stitches from the cable needle. This is called "cable 6 front." Finally, purl the last two stitches.

To work a panel of cable that crosses from left to right: Purl the first two stitches, then slip the next three stitches onto a cable needle and leave them at the back of the work.

Knit the next three stitches, then knit the stitches from the cable needle. This is called "cable 6 back." Finally, purl the last two stitches.

Coral Mula

Geometry lesson

Squares, stripes and rectangles combine to make this child's colorful pullover. The left shoulder is fastened with bright matching buttons.

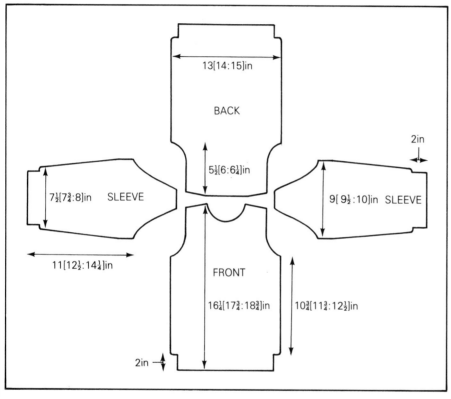

John Hutchinson

13[14:15]in

BACK

5½[6:6¼]in

7½[7¾:8]in SLEEVE

9[9½:10]in SLEEVE

2in

11[12½:14¼]in

FRONT

16¼[17¾:18¾]in   10¾[11¾:12½]in

2in

Sizes
To fit 24[26:28]in (61[66:71]cm) chest. Length, 16¼[17¾:18¾]in (41[45:48]cm). Sleeve seam, 11[12½:14¼]in (28[32:36]cm).
Note Directions for the larger sizes are in brackets [ ]; where there is one set of figures it applies to all sizes.

Gauge
22 sts and 30 rows to 4in (10cm) in st st on No. 6 (4mm) needles.

Materials
4[4:6]oz (100[100:150]g) of knitting worsted yarn each in main color (A) and contrasting color (B)
2oz (50g) each in contrasting colors (C and D)
One pair each No. 4 (3½mm) and No. 6 (4mm) knitting needles
3 bright buttons

Note Do not carry yarn across the back of the work. Use separate balls when required, twisting the yarn on the wrong side of work when changing colors to avoid a hole.

Back
Using No. 4 (3½mm) needles and A, cast on 66[72:78] sts. Work in K1, P1, ribbing for 2in (5cm).
Inc row Rib 7[8:9], lift strand running from base of st just worked to base of next st onto LH needle and work into back of it – called M1—, (rib 13[14:15], M1) 4 times, rib 7[8:9]. 71[77:83] sts. Change to No. 6 (4mm) needles and work in patt as foll:*
1st row Join in B and K48[51:55], K23[26:28] A.
2nd row P23[26:28] A. P48[51:55] A.
Rep these 2 rows until back measures approx 8¼[9½:10¼]in (21[24:26]cm) from beg, ending with a WS row. Break off

both colors. Join in C and, starting with a K row, work 12 rows in st st. Break off C and work as foll:
Next row Using A K14[15:16], K9[10:11] B, K48[52:56] D.
Next row P48[52:56] D, P9[10:11] B, P14[15:16] A.
Rep these 2 rows until back measures 10¾[11¾:12½]in (27[30:32]cm) from beg, ending with a WS row.
Shape armholes
Keeping patt correct, bind off 4 sts at beg of next 2 rows. Dec 1 st at each end of next 3 rows, dec 1 st at each end of every foll other row until 53[57:61] sts rem. Work even until armhole measures 5½[6:6¼]in (14[15:16]cm) from beg, ending with a WS row.
Shape shoulders
Bind off 5 sts at beg of next 4 rows. Bind off 4[5:6] sts at beg of next 2 rows. Leave rem 25[27:29] sts on spare needle.

Front
Work patt as given for back to *, then work colored patt as foll:
1st row Join in A and K48[51:55], K23[26:28] B.
2nd row P23[26:28] B, P48[51:55] A.
Rep these 2 rows until front measures 8¼[9½:10¼]in (21[24:26]cm) from beg ending with a WS row. Break off both colors. Join in C and, starting with a K row, work 12 rows in st st. Break off C and work as foll:
Next row Using A K14[15:16], K9[10:11] B, K48[52:56] A.
Next row P48[52:56] A, P9[10:11] B, P14[15:16] A.
Rep these 2 rows until front measures 10¾[11¾:12½]in (27[30:32]cm) from beg, ending with a WS row. Cont working as for back until front is 16 rows shorter than back to start of shoulder shaping, ending with a WS row.
Shape neck
Next row Keeping patt correct, K18[19:20], K2 tog, turn and leave rem sts on a spare needle.
Dec 1 st at neck edge on next 2 rows, then dec 1 st at neck edge on every other row 3 times. 14[15:16] sts.
Work even until front measures same as

back to start of shoulder shaping, ending with a WS row.

Shape shoulder
Bind off 5 sts at beg of next 4 rows. Bind off 4[5:6] sts.

Shape second side of neck
With RS facing, sl next 13[15:17] sts onto a spare needle, rejoin yarn to rem 20[21:22] sts, patt 2 tog, patt to end. Work to match first side reversing shapings.

Right sleeve
Using No. 4 (3½mm) needles and B, cast on 36[38:40] sts and work in K1, P1 ribbing for 2in (5cm).
Inc row Rib 4[5:4], M1, (rib 7[7:8], M1) 4 times, rib 4[5:4]. 41[43:45] sts. Change to No. 6 (4mm) needles and, starting with a K row, work 6 rows in st st. Cont in st st, inc 1 st at each end of next and every foll 15th[14th:17th] row, until there are 49[53:55] sts. Work even until sleeve measures 8½[10¼:11¾]in (22[26:30]cm) from beg, ending with a P row. Break off B. Join in C and, starting with a K row, work 12 rows in st st. Break off C. Join in A and, starting with a K row, work in st st until sleeve seam measures 11[12½:14¼]in (28[32:36]cm) from beg, ending with WS row.

Shape armholes
Bind off 4 sts at beg of next 2 rows. Dec 1 st at each end of next and every foll 4th row until 33[39:41] sts rem. Work 3 rows even. Now dec 1 st at each end of next and every other row until 13 sts rem, ending with a WS row. Bind off.

Left sleeve
Work as given for right sleeve, using A in place of B, and D in place of A. (C rem the same.)

Buttonhole band
Using No. 4 (3½mm) needles and D, starting at armhole edge of front shoulder seam, pick up and K 23[25:27] sts. Work 3 rows in P1, K1 ribbing.
Next row Rib 2, (bind off next 3 sts, rib 6) twice, bind off next 3 sts, rib 2.
Next row. Work in ribbing, casting on 3 sts over those bound off in previous row. Work 2 more rows in ribbing.
Bind off evenly in ribbing.

Neckband
Join right shoulder seam. Using No. 4 (3½mm) needles and D, pick up and K14 sts down left side of neck, K across 13[15:17] sts at center front, pick up and K14 sts up right side of neck, K across 25[27:29] sts, inc 1 st at center back neck. 67[71:75] sts. Work in K1, P1, ribbing for 1¼in. Bind off.

To finish
Do not press. Join side and sleeve seams. Insert sleeves, joining edge of band to sleeve edge at armhole. Sew on buttons to correspond with buttonholes.

The well-dressed baby kit (1)

What could be more satisfying than to knit a complete ward-robe for a baby? This beautiful collection in a lacy stitch is sized for a three- to six-month-old infant. Directions for the blanket, the dress, the angel top and the buttoned jacket are given here; the next chaper includes directions for the other garments.

Peter Pugh-Cook

Sizes

To fit 3-6 months.
Blanket size : 45in (114cm) square.

Tension

30 sts to 4in (10cm) in patt worked on
No. 3 (3¼mm) needles.

Materials

A sport yarn
Blanket: 15oz (400g)
Dress: 4oz (100g)
Angel Top: 4oz (100g)
Jacket: 4oz (100g)
One pair Nos. 1, 2, 3 and 6 (2¾, 3, 3¼, 4½mm) knitting needles
3 small buttons for dress
3 small buttons for angel top
4 small buttons for jacket

Blanket

Using No. 6 (4½mm) needles cast on
243 sts. Begin patt.
1st row K2, *sl 1, K1, psso, K3, yo, K1, yo, K3, K2 tog, K1, rep from * to last st, K1.
2nd row P2, *P2 tog, P2, yo, P3, yo, P2, P2 tbl, P1, rep from * to last st, P1.
3rd row K2, *sl 1, K1, psso, K1, yo, K5, yo, K1, K2 tog, K1, rep from * to last st, K1.
4th row P2, *yo, P2 tog, P7, P2 tbl, yo, P1, rep from * to last st, P1.
5th row K2, *yo, K3, K2 tog, K1, sl 1,

K1, psso, K3, yo, K1, rep from * to last st, K1.
6th row P3, *yo, P2, P2 tbl, P1, P2 tog, P2, yo, P3, rep from * to end.
7th row K4, *yo, K1, K2 tog, K1, sl 1, K1, psso, K1, yo, K5, rep from * to end but finish last rep K4 instead of K5.
8th row P5, *P2 tbl, yo, P1, yo, P2 tog, P7, rep from * to end but finish last rep P5 instead of P7.
These 8 rows form the patt. Cont in patt until the 8th row of the 41st patt has been worked. Bind off.

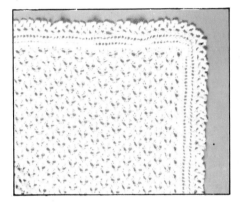

Edging

Using No. 6 (4½mm) needles cast on
11 sts. K one row. Begin patt.
1st row K3, (yo, sl 1, K1, psso, K1) twice, (yo) twice, K1, (yo) twice, K1, 15 sts.

2nd row (K2, P1) 4 times, K3, (note that on this row each double yo is worked as 2 sts, the first being knitted and the second being purled). 15 sts.
3rd row K3, yo, sl 1, K1, psso, K1, yo, sl 1, K1, psso, K7, 15sts.
4th row Bind off 4 sts, K4, P1, K2, P1, K3, 11 sts.
These 4 rows form the patt. Cont in patt until edging fits all around outer edge of main piece, allowing an extra 1½in (4cm) at each corner, ending with a 4th row. Bind off.

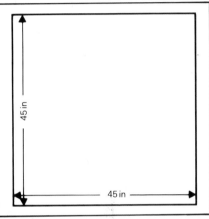

To finish

Join cast-on and bound-off edges of edging together. Sew edging to main piece, easing it in at corners. Roll in a damp cloth. Lay flat and leave to dry.

Dress

Using No. 3 (3¼mm) needles cast on
243 sts and work in one piece to underarm. Work 7 rows garter st. Proceed in patt as given for blanket until work measures 8½in (21.5cm) from beg. End with 8th row.
Divide for armholes
Next row Patt 63, bind off 2 sts, patt until there are 113 sts on right-hand needle after bound off group, bind off 2 sts, patt to end.
Keeping patt correct, dec one st at armhole edge on next 7 rows. 56 sts. Cut off yarn and leave sts on holder.
With WS of work facing, rejoin yarn to front sts, keeping patt correct dec one st at each end of next 7 rows, 99 sts. Cut off yarn and leave sts on holder.
With WS of work facing, rejoin yarn to rem sts and complete to match right back, reversing shaping. Do not cut off yarn but leave sts on holder.
Sleeves
Using No. 1 (2¾mm) needles cast on
49 sts. Work 3 rows garter st.
Next row K4, *inc in next st, K2, rep from * to last 3 sts, K3. 51 sts. Change to No. 3 (3¼mm) needles. Work 8 rows patt, inc one st at end of last row. 52 sts.
Shape top
Keeping patt correct, bind off 2 sts at beg

of next 2 rows, then dec one st at each end of next 5 rows, 38 sts. Work one row. Cut off yarn and leave sts on holder.

Kim Sayer

Yoke

Using No. 2 (3mm) needles and with RS of work facing, work across sts on holders as foll:
Next row K6, (K2 tog) 25 times across left back ; K2 tog, K34, K2 tog, across left sleeve, K4, (K2 tog) 45 times, K5 across front ; K2 tog, K34, K2 tog, across right sleeve ; (K2 tog) 27 times, K2 across right back; turn; cast on 6 sts for underflap, 192 sts. Work 11 rows garter st.
Next row (buttonhole row) K1, K2 tog, yo, K3, *K1, K2 tog, rep from * to last 6 sts, K6. 132 sts.
Work 11 rows garter st.

Next row (buttonhole row) K1, K2 tog, yo, K3, *K1, K2 tog, rep from * to last 6 sts, K6, 92 sts.
Work 7 rows garter st.
Next row K7, *K2 tog, K1, rep from * to last 7 sts, K7, 66 sts.
Next 2 rows K11, turn, sl 1, K to end.
Next 2 rows K22, turn, sl 1, K to end.
K one row across all sts.
Next 2 rows K11, turn, sl 1, K to end.
Next 2 rows K22, turn, sl 1, K to end.
Change to No. 1 (2¾mm) needles. Work 5 rows garter st making buttonhole as before at beg of 3rd row. Bind off loosely.

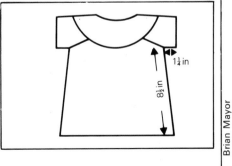

Brian Mayor

To finish Join sleeve and underarm seams. Join back to underflap. Sew down underflap. Sew on buttons.

Angel top

Work as for dress until skirt measures 7in (18cm); work armholes as for dress.

Sleeves

Using No. 1 (2½mm) needles cast on 32 sts. Work 3 rows garter st.

Next row K6, *inc in next st, rep from * to last 7 sts, K7, 51 sts. Change to No. 3 (3¼mm) needles. Proceed in patt until work measures 5½in (14cm), ending with an 8th row (inc one st in last row), 52 sts.

Shape top

Keeping patt correct, bind off 2 sts at beg. of next 2 rows, then dec one st at each end of next 5 rows. 38 sts. Work one row. Cut off yarn and leave sts on holder. Finish as for dress.

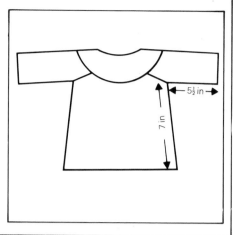

Jacket

Using No. 3 (3¼mm) needles cast on 243 sts and work in one piece to underarm. Work 7 rows garter st. Proceed in patt as given for blanket, working 6 sts at each end on every row in garter st until work measures 7in (18cm) from beg. End with an 8th row.

Divide for armholes

Next row K6, patt 57, bind off 2, patt until there are 113 sts on right-hand needle after bound-off group, bind off 2, patt to last 6 sts, K6.

Complete left front first. Keeping patt and garter st border correct, dec one st at armhole edge on next 7 rows, 56 sts. Cut off yarn and leave sts on holder. With WS of work facing, rejoin yarn to back sts and keeping patt correct dec one st at each end of next 7 rows, 99 sts. Cut off yarn and leave sts on holder. With WS of work facing, rejoin yarn to right front sts and complete to match left front reversing shaping. Do not cut off yarn but leave sts on holder.

Sleeves

Work as given for sleeves of angel top.

Yoke

Using No. 2 (3mm) needles and with RS of work facing, work across all sts on holders as foll:

Next row K1, K2 tog, yo, K3, (K2 tog)

23 times, K4 across right front, K2 tog, K34, K2 tog across right sleeve, K4, (K2 tog) 45 times, K5 across back, K2 tog, K34, K2 tog across left sleeve, K4, (K2 tog) 23 times, K6 across left front, 192 sts.

Work 11 rows garter st.

Next row (buttonhole row) K1, K2 tog, yfwd, K3, *K1, K2 tog, rep from * to last 6 sts, K6, 132 sts.

Work 11 rows garter st.

Next row (buttonhole row) K1, K2 tog, yo, K3, *K1, K2 tog, rep from * to last 6 sts, K6, 92 sts.

Work 7 rows garter st.

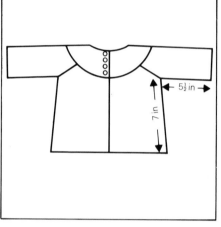

Next row K7, *K2 tog, K1, rep from * to last 7 sts, K7, 66 sts.

Next 2 rows K to last 11 sts, turn, sl 1, K to last 11 sts, turn.

Next 2 rows Sl 1, K to last 18 sts, turn, sl 1, K to last 18 sts, turn.

Next row Sl 1, K to end of row. Change to No. 1 (2½mm) needles. Work 5 rows garter st making buttonhole as before at beg of 3rd row. Bind off loosely.

To finish

Join sleeve and underarm seams. Sew on buttons.

Technique tip

Working a yoke

The angel top, dress and jacket in this collection have a yoke that is worked all in one piece. This is very common in babies' garments, as it eliminates the need for any bulky seams. In these garments the main piece is worked all in one to the top of the skirt. The work is then divided and the armhole shaping is worked on each piece and the stitches are then left on holders to be worked on at a later stage. The sleeves are knitted next and left on holders, then all the stitches are knitted from the holders in the appropriate order, depending on the pattern.

To shape the yoke, you need to decrease stitches across a number of rows. The decreases are worked across the row to give an even shape and should be spaced evenly so that they form a feature of the garment rather than looking haphazard.

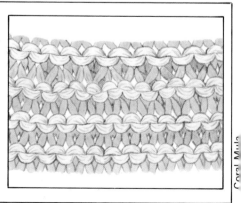

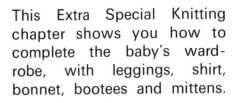

This Extra Special Knitting chapter shows you how to complete the baby's wardrobe, with leggings, shirt, bonnet, bootees and mittens.

The well-dressed baby kit (2)

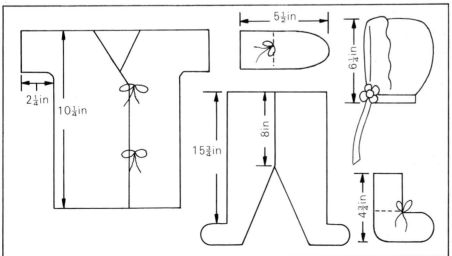

Jerry Tubby

John Hutchinson

Sizes
To fit 3–6 months.

Materials

Sport yarn
Leggings 4oz (100g)
Shirt 4oz (100g)
Bonnet, bootees and mittens 2oz (50g)
1 pair No. 2 (2¾mm) and 1 pair No. 3 (3¼mm) knitting needles
1¾yd (1.5m) narrow ribbon for shirt
2¼yd (2m) of 1in (2.5cm)-wide ribbon for bonnet
2¼yd (2m) of narrow ribbon for bootees and mittens
Elastic cord for leggings

Gauge
30 sts to 4in (10cm) in patt worked on No. 3 (3¼mm) needles.

Leggings

Right leg

**Using No. 2 (2¾mm) needles cast on 73 sts.
1st row K1, (P1, K1) to end.
2nd row P1, (K1, P1) to end.
Rep these 2 rows 4 times more. Change to No. 3 (3¼mm) needles.

Shape back

Next 2 rows Work 16, turn, sl 1, work to end.
Next 2 rows Work 24, turn, sl 1, work to end.
Next 2 rows Work 32, turn, sl 1, work to end.
Cont shaping in this way until the row "work 56, turn, sl 1, work to end" has been worked. Cont in stockinette st but inc one st at each end of 3rd and every following 10th row until there are 81 sts in all. Cont without shaping until work measures 8in (20cm) from beg, ending with a P row.

Shape leg

Bind off 3 sts at beg of next 2 rows, then dec one st at each end of next and every foll 3rd row until 39 sts rem. Cont without shaping until work measures 8in (20cm) from beg of leg shaping (measured on the straight), ending with a P row.**

Shape instep

1st row K29, K2 tog, turn.
2nd row P13, turn.
Work 28 rows stockinette st on these 13 sts for instep, dec one st at end of last row. 12 sts.
Cut off yarn. With RS of work facing, pick up and K 14 sts along side of instep, K across instep sts, pick up and K 14 sts along other side of instep and K across sts one left-hand needle. 65 sts.
Work 15 rows garter st.

Shape foot

1st row K2, K2 tog, K1, K2 tog, K27, K2 tog, K2, K2 tog, K25.
2nd row K to end.
3rd row K1, K2 tog, K1, K2 tog, K25, K2 tog, K2, K2 tog, K24.
4th row K to end.
5th row K28, K2 tog, K2, K2 tog, K23.
6th row K to end. Bind off loosely.

Left leg

Work as given for right leg from ** to ** but reverse shaping by knitting one row before shaping back.

Shape instep

1st row K20, K2 tog, turn.
2nd row P13, turn.
Work 28 rows stockinette st on these 13 sts for instep, dec one st at end of last row. 12 sts.
Cut off yarn. With WS of work facing, pick up and K 14 sts along side of instep, K across instep sts, pick up 14 stockinette st along other side of instep and K across 17 sts on left-hand needle. 65 sts. Work 15 rows garter st.

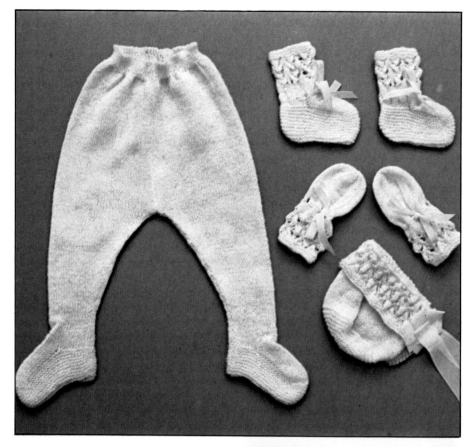

Shape foot

1st row K25, K2 tog, K2, K2 tog, K27, K2 tog, K1, K2 tog, K2.
2nd row K to end.
3rd row K24, K2 tog, K2 K2 tog, K25, K2 tog, K1, K2 tog, K1.
4th row K to end.
5th row K23, K2 tog, K2, K2 tog, K28.
6th row K to end. Bind off loosely.

To finish

Block according to yarn used, pressing lightly. Join front, back and leg seams. Beg at center of toe, join foot seam. With WS of work facing, thread elastic through every K st on first and every other row of ribbing at waist edge.

Shirt

Using No. 3 (3¼mm) needles cast on 64 sts for lower edge of back.
Work 5 rows garter st.
Beg with a K row, proceed in stockinette st until work measures 6in (15cm) from beg, ending with a P row. Inc one st at each end of next and every other row until there are 72 sts, ending with a P row.

Shaping sleeves

Cast on 10 sts at beg of next 2 rows. 92 sts.
Next row K to end.
Next row K4, P to last 4 sts, K4.
Rep last 2 rows until work measures 10in (25cm) from beg, ending with a K row.
Next row K4, P29, K26, P29, K4.
Next row K to end.
Rep last 2 rows twice more.

Divide for neck

Next row K4, P29, K4, turn and leave rem sts on holder.
Next row K4, inc in next st, K to end.
Next row K4, P to last 4 sts, K4.
Cont in this way inc one st at front

edge inside border on 11th row, then on every alternate row until sleeve edge measures 7in (17.5cm), ending at side edge. Bind off 10 sts at beg of next row for sleeve. Continue to inc at front edge as before, **at the same time** dec one st at armhole edge on next and every alternate row 4 times in all. Keeping armhole edge straight, continue to inc at front edge until there are 45 sts. Continue without shaping, keeping front border correct, until work measures same as back to top of waistband, ending with a K row. Work 4 rows garter st. Bind off.

With WS of work facing, rejoin yarn to, rem sts, bind off 18 sts for center neck, work to end of row. Complete to match first side, reversing shaping.

To finish
Join side and sleeve seams. Overlap right front over left front and sew on ribbons to last shaping and 2in (5cm) below.

Bonnet
Using No. 3 (3¼mm) needles cast on 87 sts. Work 4 rows garter st. Begin patt.
1st row K2, *sl 1, K1, psso, K3, yo, K1, yo, K3, K2 tog, K1, rep from * to last st, K1.
2nd row P2, *P2 tog, P2, yo, P3, yo, P2, P2 tog, tbl, P1, rep from * to last st, P1.
3rd row K2, *sl 1, K1, psso, K1, yo, K5, yo, K1, K2 tog, K1, rep from * to last st, K1.
4th row P2, *yo, P2 tog, P7, P2 tog tbl, yo, P1, rep from * to last st, P1.
5th row K2, *yo, K3, K2 tog, K1, sl 1, K1, psso, K3, yo, K1, rep from * to last st, K1.
6th row P3, *yo, P2, P2 tog tbl, P1, P2 tog, P2, yo, P3, rep from * to end.
7th row K4, *yo, K1, K2 tog, K1, sl 11, K1, psso, K1, yo, K5, rep from * to end but finish last rep K4 instead of K5.
8th row P5, *P2 tog tbl, yo, P1, yo, P2 tog, P7, rep from * to end but finish last rep P5 instead of P7.
These 8 rows form the patt. Rep them once more. Work 4 rows garter st.
1st rib row K1, (P1, K1) to end.
2nd rib row P1, (K1, P1) to end.
Rep these 2 rows 3 times more, then work 1st rib row again.
Beg with a K row, proceed in stockinette st until work measures 6¼in (16cm) from beg, ending with a P row and inc 3 sts evenly across last row.
Work 4 row garter st.

Shape for crown
1st row *K7, K2 tog, rep from * to end. 80 sts.
2nd and every alternate row K to end.
3rd row *K6, K2 tog, rep from * to end. 70 sts.
5th row *K5, K2 tog, rep from * to end. 60 sts.
Continue dec in this way until 10 sts rem. Cut off yarn, thread through rem sts, draw up and secure.

To finish
Join back seam to beg of shaping. Turn back brim.
Neck edge Using No. 2 (2¾mm) needles and with RS of work facing pick up 81 sts around neck, working through double thickness at brim.
Beg with 2nd rib row, work 6 rows. Bind off.
Make 2 ribbon rosettes, leaving rem ribbon free to tie, and sew one to each side of bonnet.

Bootees
**Using No. 3 (3¼mm) needles cast on 39 sts. Work 5 rows garter st.
Work 16 rows patt as given for bonnet.
Beg with a K row, work 6 rows stockinette st, inc one st at end of last row. 40 sts.
Next row *K2, yo, K2 tog, rep from * to end.
Next row P to end.**
Next row K7, (K2 tog, K9) 3 times.
Next row P to end.
Divide for instep
1st row K24, turn.
2nd row P11, turn.
Work 20 rows stockinette st on these 11 sts for instep. Cut off yarn. With RS of work facing, pick up 14 sts along side of instep, K across instep sts, pick up 14 sts along other side of instep and K across 13 sts on left-hand needle. 65 sts.
Work 15 rows garter st.
Shape foot
1st row K2 tog, K25, K2 tog, K7, K2 tog, K25, K2 tog.
2nd and every alternate row K to end.
3rd row K2 tog, K24, K2 tog, K5, K2 tog, K24, K2 tog.
5th row K2 tog, K23, K2 tog, K3, K2 tog, K23, K2 tog.
7th row K2 tog, K22, K2 tog, K1, K2 tog, K22, K2 tog.
8th row K to end. Bind off loosely.

To finish
Join foot and leg seams. Thread ribbon through eyelet holes and tie with a bow at center front.

Mittens
Work as given for bootees from **to**
Continue in stockinette st until work measures 2⅜in (6cm) from eyelet hole row.

Shape top
1st row *K2, K2 tog, rep from *to end.
2nd row P to end.
3rd row *K1, K2 tog, rep from *to end.
4th row P to end.
5th row *K2 tog, rep from *to end.
Cut off yarn, thread end through stitches, draw up tightly and secure.

To finish
Join seams. Thread ribbon through eyelet holes and tie with a bow at center front.

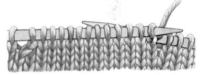

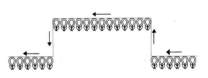

EXTRA SPECIAL SEWING

Fake it in suede

Spot the difference if you can! This imitation suede fabric is a marvelous, inexpensive way of looking really classy — and it's fully washable, too.

Measurements

Finished length, 24¼in (61.5cm).
Shown here is size 12, the pattern can be adjusted to fit sizes 10–16.
A ⅝in (1.5cm) seam allowance is included where necessary.

Note It is possible to draw the pattern sections directly on the fabric with chalk, but we recommend making a paper pattern from the diagrams.

Materials

- 1⅛yd (1m) of 45in (114cm)-wide imitation suede fabric
- Matching thread
- Two 1⅛in (28mm) button forms or two 1⅛in (28mm) diameter buttons for belted version
- Tracing paper, brown paper or tissue paper
- Chalk, yardstick, pencil
- Transparent tape

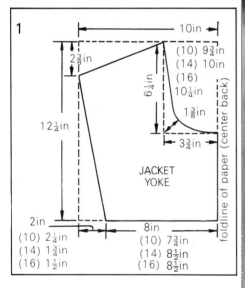

1 Make a paper pattern piece for the yoke. Take a piece of paper 19¾ × 12¼in (50 × 31cm) and fold it in half so that you have a folded piece 12¼ × 10in (31 × 25cm). Mark the measurements for you size as shown (we have made the jacket in size 12; sizes 10, 14 and 16 are in parenthesis where the measurements vary). To make the neck edge (same size for all sizes), mark the measurement lines, then sketch in the curve. The curve should be 1⅜in (3.5cm) from the measured right angle.

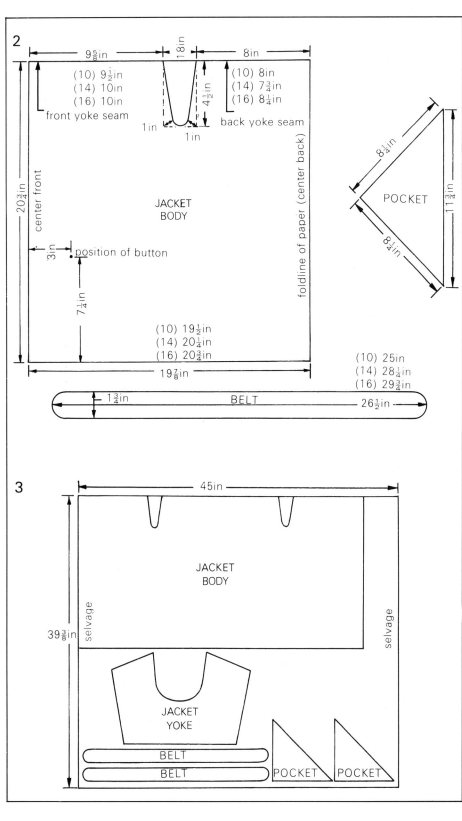

2 The main pattern piece

2 (10) $9\frac{1}{2}$in
(14) 10in
(16) 10in
front yoke seam

$9\frac{5}{8}$in

$1\frac{1}{8}$in

8in

(10) 8in
(14) $7\frac{3}{4}$in
(16) $8\frac{1}{4}$in
back yoke seam

$4\frac{1}{2}$in

1in   1in

P

$20\frac{3}{4}$in   center front

JACKET
BODY

foldline of paper (center back)

POCKET

$8\frac{1}{4}$in

$8\frac{1}{4}$in

$11\frac{3}{4}$in

3in   position of button

$7\frac{1}{4}$in

(10) $19\frac{1}{2}$in
(14) $20\frac{1}{4}$in
(16) $20\frac{3}{4}$in

$19\frac{7}{8}$in

(10) 25in
(14) $28\frac{1}{4}$in
(16) $29\frac{3}{4}$in

$1\frac{3}{4}$in   BELT $26\frac{1}{2}$in

3   45in

JACKET
BODY

selvage   selvage

$39\frac{3}{8}$in

JACKET
YOKE

BELT

BELT

POCKET   POCKET

2 For the main pattern piece you will need a piece of paper $39\frac{3}{4} \times 20\frac{3}{4}$in (101 × 52.5cm). Fold it in half so that you have a folded piece $19\frac{7}{8} \times 20\frac{3}{4}$in (50.5 × 52.5cm). Follow the same principle for making the armhole shape as for the neckline. Use scraps of paper to make patterns for the belt or pockets, following the measurements on the diagram.

3 Trim off selvages; then following pattern layout, cut out one body section, one yoke and the belt or pockets—depending on the version you are making—following the measurements on the diagram.
Mark button positions with tailor's chalk.

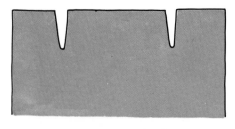

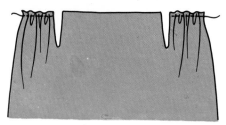

4 Starting 2in (5cm) from center front edge of body section and finishing 2in (5cm) from armhole edge, work a line of gathering stitches inside seam allowance. Repeat for other side. Pull up gathers.

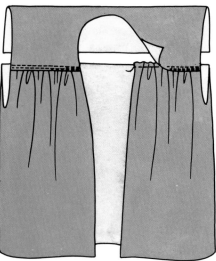

5 Matching armhole edges, lap yoke $\frac{5}{8}$in (1.5cm) over both sides of the body front (wrong side of yoke laps over right side fronts). Adjust gathers to fit yoke and secure. Baste and make a double line of topstitching on each yoke seam.

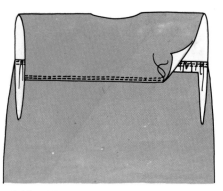

6 Matching side edges, lap back yoke $\frac{5}{8}$in (1.5cm) over back of body section. Baste and topstitch back yoke seam.

7 For the belted version cover two button forms with suede fabric, following the directions on the package. Sew buttons in place on the body section fronts, in positions marked.

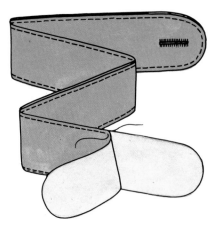

8 Place one belt section on top of the other, wrong sides together. Topstitch all around, $\frac{1}{4}$in (6mm) from the edge. Work a horizontal buttonhole at both ends of belt, starting 1in (2.5cm) in from each end of belt. Button belt to vest.

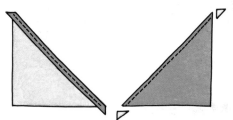

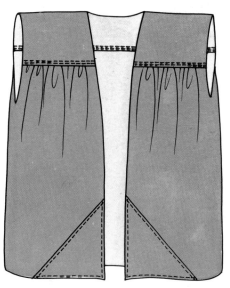

9 For pocket version, turn under a $\frac{3}{8}$in (1cm) hem on diagonal edge of each pocket and topstitch $\frac{1}{4}$in (6mm) from fold. Trim seam allowances at corners. Position pockets on vest as shown and topstitch remaining edges of pocket $\frac{1}{4}$in (6mm) from raw edges.

Technique tip

Working with suede fabric

There are different types of imitation suede on the market, and for this pattern it is very important to use one that is the same on both sides (fully reversible). Do not attempt to use a fabric with a cloth backing; it will not have enough body.

Cutting out

The fabric has a nap, so all pattern pieces must lie in the same direction on the fabric layout. Mark the fabric on the wrong side.

Handling the suede fabric

Avoid pinning, as pins leave holes in the fabric. Instead use a piece of transparent tape to hold the seams together on the wrong side and peel it off after stitching. Use fine needles for hand sewing and basting. To prevent the fabric from sticking as you sew, replace your normal machine foot with a roller foot if possible; otherwise, dust the fabric lightly with talcum powder as you sew.

Use a medium stitch and either cotton or synthetic thread in the machine. Experiment with a scrap of fabric to see which is more suitable.

Seaming

To avoid bulk use adapted flat fell seams. Lap one edge $\frac{5}{8}$in (1.5cm) over the other.

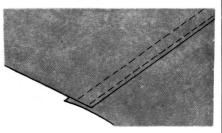

Topstitch $\frac{1}{8}$in (3mm) from outer edge of upper layer. Make a second row of topstitching $\frac{1}{4}$in (6mm) from the first.

Mix and match smock: directions for making (1)

Team them up or wear them separately. This smock and skirt will suit all seasons, depending on the fabric you select. In this chapter we tell you how to make the smock; directions for the skirt will be given on page 100.

Measurements

To fit sizes 10 to 14
Finished length of smock 32in (81cm)
Finished length of skirt, $33\frac{3}{4}$in (86cm)

Materials

For matching smock and skirt:
   $4\frac{5}{8}$yd (4.2m) fabric
For smock:
   $2\frac{1}{2}$yd (2.2m) fabric
For skirt:
   $2\frac{1}{4}$yd (2m) fabric
Matching thread
Two $\frac{5}{8}$in (1.5cm) diameter buttons (smock)
$1\frac{1}{8}$yd (1m) of $\frac{1}{4}$in (6mm)-wide elastic (skirt)
8in (20cm) seam binding
Tailor's chalk
Flexible curve

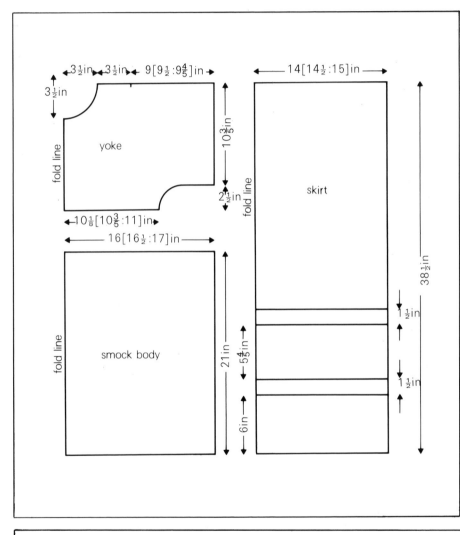

Terry Evans

Note You'll find a flexible curve helpful in getting the correct shapes for the under-arm seam and neckline on the smock and also in drawing other curves on garments in future chapters. It is a plastic-covered piece of wire (available from art supply shops), which can be bent to any curved shape and remains firm while you draw around it.

1 Cutting the yoke section will be easier if you first make a paper pattern. Take a piece of tissue or brown paper $13\frac{1}{4} \times$ 33in (33.5×84cm) and fold it in half so that you have a double piece $13\frac{1}{4} \times 16\frac{1}{2}$in (33.5×42cm). Using a flexible curve, draw the curves for the neckline and underarm edges following the shapes on the diagram and the measurements for your size. Measure and cut out the smock body and the skirt directly on the folded fabric.

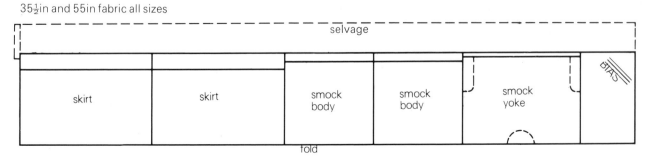

Brian Mayor

2 Open paper yoke piece and pin it on the fabric, with shoulder line on folded edge. Cut out the yoke. Cut out two smock body sections to the measurements given for your size; two bias strips $1\frac{1}{2} \times 21\frac{5}{8}$in ($4 \times 55$cm) for the neck binding; and two bias strips $1\frac{1}{2} \times 2\frac{3}{4}$in ($4 \times 7$cm) for the button loops. A $\frac{5}{8}$in (1.5cm) seam allowance and a $\frac{3}{8}$in (1cm) hem allowance are included.

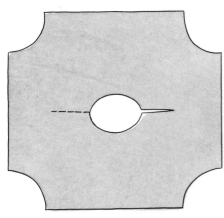

3 Open out the yoke section and mark a $3\frac{1}{2}$in (9cm)-long line with tailor's chalk on each side of the neckline, as shown. Cut along lines.

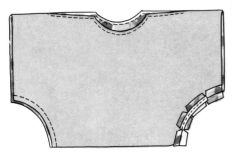

4 Staystitch along neck slits and around neck curve to prevent fraying. With right sides together and raw edges even, pin, baste and stitch underarm seams. Clip curves and press seams open. Reinforce seam by basting and stitching a 4in (10cm) length of seam binding over seam at underarm, as shown.

5 With right sides together and raw edges even, pin, baste and stitch smock body side seams. Press seams open. Run two lines of gathering stitches around the top edge.

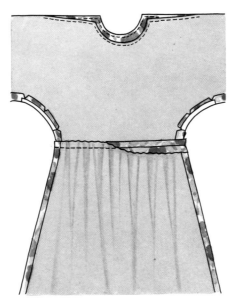

6 Pull up gathering threads until the smock body fits the lower edge of the yoke. With right sides together, pin yoke to body, matching side seams. Distribute the gathers evenly all around. Baste and stitch smock yoke to smock body. Press seam allowance toward yoke. Turn the smock right side out.

7 Apply the button loops and bias strips to smock neck edge and slits.
8 Fold under and baste a $\frac{1}{4}$in (6mm) hem on lower edge of sleeve. Fold under a further $\frac{1}{4}$in (6mm), baste and stitch to make a double hem. Repeat for second sleeve and lower edge of smock adjusting the length if you wish.

Technique tip

Button loops and bias edging

Stitch the two short bias strips along their long edges and turn them right side out to make tubes.
Fold each length in half and pin it to one side of the yoke with its raw edges at corner of neck slit, as shown. Position the other loop at the other corner of neck.
Turn under $\frac{1}{4}$in (6mm) at one end of one neckline bias strip and, with right sides together and raw edges even, pin and baste it to the back neckline edge, starting at the end of one neckline slit and mitering the corners at the neck. Turn under the free

end of the strip $\frac{1}{4}$in (6mm), trimming excess if necessary, before basting this end in place. Stitch close to raw edges and press binding and seam allowance upward.
Turn binding to wrong side, turn under a tiny hem and hand stitch to wrong side of neck edge along line of stitching. Repeat on the front neck edge, basting and stitching the binding over the button loops, then turning it to the wrong side to finish. Reinforce the ends of neckline slits with buttonhole stitch.

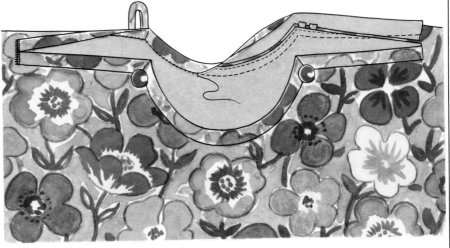

Terry Evans

99

Mix and match (2)

Note Shorten or lengthen the skirt at the waistline so that the position of the tucks remains the same.

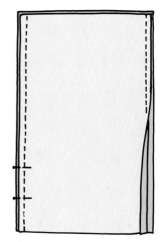

1 Cut out two skirt sections to the correct measurements for your size. Make tailor's tacks to mark the positions of tuck lines.

With right sides together and raw edges even, pin, baste and stitch side seams.

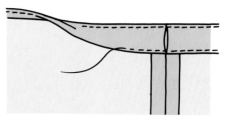

2 On wrong side, fold and baste a $\frac{1}{4}$in (6mm) hem to inside at waist edge. Fold over $\frac{3}{4}$in (2cm). Stitch close to edges.

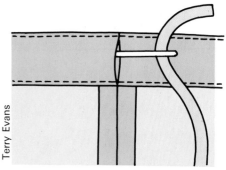

Terry Evans

3 Leave a $1\frac{1}{2}$in (4cm) opening at one of the side seams for inserting elastic. Turn skirt right side out.

Cut a length of elastic to fit your waist comfortably. Using a yarn needle, thread the elastic through the waistline casing.

To help you complete your smock and skirt twosome we now show you how to make the tucked skirt. The measurements and cutting layout are given on page 97.

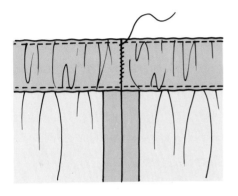

4 Try on the skirt and adjust so that it fits comfortably, bearing in mind that you may want to wear a blouse tucked into it. Tie the two elastic ends in a firm knot and slip stitch casing opening closed, leaving the knot inside. If preferred, fold the ends of the elastic over each other and stitch to make a firm join.

5 Baste and stitch tucks. Fold and bast a $\frac{1}{4}$in (6mm) hem at the lower edge, then fold and stitch a further $\frac{1}{4}$in (6mm) hem to make a double-stitched hem.

Technique tips

Making tucks

Usually tucks are put in before the garment sections are stitched together, but when you are making horizontal tucks all around a garment (as on this skirt), you must do them after joining the side seams, so that the tucks will remain free. To mark the tuck lines with tailor's tacks, measure $4\frac{3}{4}$in (12cm) up from the lower raw edge of the skirt and make your first line of tacks — at 6in (15cm) intervals — all the way around. Make another line of tacks $\frac{3}{4}$in (2cm) above the first, then another $\frac{3}{4}$in (2cm) above that. Measure $5\frac{3}{4}$in (14.5cm) up toward the waist and make a line of tacks, then two more lines, spaced as before.

Following the lines of tailor's tacks all the way around and working on the right side of the fabric, make a fold along the center line and bring the upper and lower rows together. Pin and baste these two rows together, making sure that the tucks are on the straight grain of the fabric. Work from right to left, with the lower edge of the skirt nearer you. Stitch. You will have a line of stitching showing on the right side, at the top of the tuck. Repeat for the second tuck. Press tucks toward the hem, with a strip of stiff paper beneath the tuck to prevent indentations in the fabric.

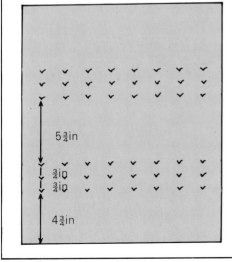

5$\frac{3}{4}$in

$\frac{3}{4}$in
$\frac{3}{4}$in

4$\frac{3}{4}$in

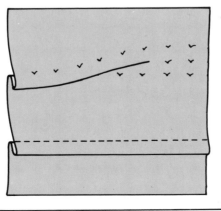

Kimono comfort

Herb Schmitz

Perfect for relaxing, these kimonos, based on a traditional Japanese design, are styled to suit men and women equally well. The woman's version is full-length and the man's is thigh-length — made in contrasting colors with added appliqué trim

Woman's kimono

Measurements (to fit sizes 10 to 16)
Finished length, 56in (142cm)
$\frac{5}{8}$in (1.5cm) seam allowances and 2in (5cm) hems on sleeves and lower edge are included in measurement diagrams.

Materials
   $4\frac{1}{4}$yd (3.8m) of 60in (150cm)-wide fabric
   $\frac{7}{8}$yd (80cm) of $\frac{5}{8}$in (1.5cm)-wide seam binding (optional)
   Tailor's chalk
   Matching thread
   Flexible curve
   Yardstick.

Note If your fabric has a one-way design, make sure that you cut out all the pieces in the same direction.

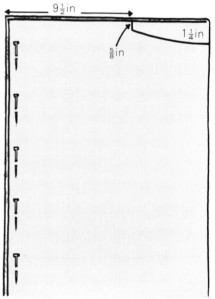

Terry Evans

1 For the back piece, cut out one rectangle, following the measurement diagram. Fold the fabric piece in half lengthwise; pin the edges even and draw the back neck curve on the fold. First mark a point 9½in (24cm) in from the raw edges and ⅝in (1.5cm) down from the upper edge. Using a flexible curve, draw a line from this point to a point 1¼in (3cm) from the top on the center fold. Keeping the fabric folded, cut out the neck curve. Remove the pins and unfold back piece.

Diagram labels: 9½in, 1¼in, ⅝in

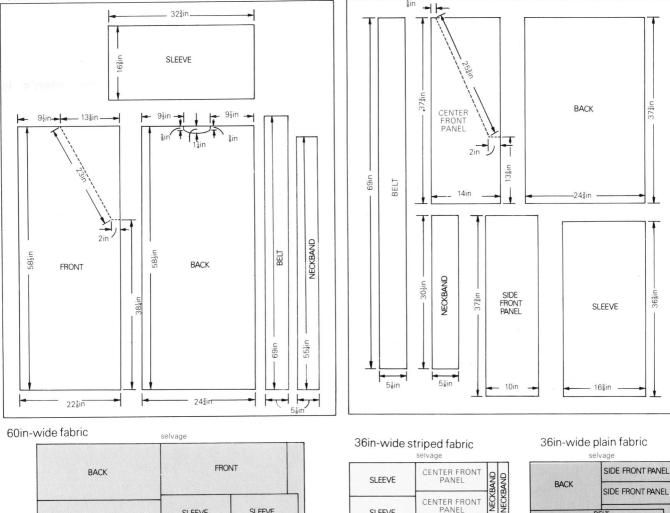

Woman's kimono

SLEEVE — 32¾in × 16⅛in

FRONT — 9½in / 13¾in, 58½in, 23in, 2in, 22⅞in

BACK — 9½in / 9½in, ⅝in, 1¼in, ⅝in, 58½in, 38¼in, 24¾in

BELT — 69in

NECKBAND — 55¼in, 5⅛in

Man's kimono

⅝in

CENTER FRONT PANEL — 37¾in, 25¼in, 2in, 14in, 13¾in

BACK — 37¾in, 24¾in, 36⅛in

BELT — 69in

NECKBAND — 30½in, 5⅛in, 5⅛in

SIDE FRONT PANEL — 37¾in, 10in

SLEEVE — 16⅛in

60in-wide fabric

selvage

BACK, FRONT, FRONT, SLEEVE, SLEEVE, NECKBAND, BELT

selvage

36in-wide striped fabric

selvage

SLEEVE, CENTER FRONT PANEL, NECKBAND, NECKBAND, SLEEVE, CENTER FRONT PANEL

selvage

36in-wide plain fabric

selvage

BACK, SIDE FRONT PANEL, SIDE FRONT PANEL, BELT

selvage

John Hutcjinson

Terry Evans

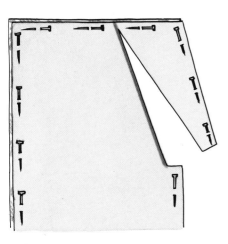

2 Cut out the two front rectangles. Place one piece on top of the other with right sides together, matching all edges. Pin. Using tailor's chalk and a yardstick, and following the measurements on the diagram, mark the front neck edge. Cut out. Unpin.

3 Cut two sleeves, one neckband, and one belt, making it wider or narrower if you wish.

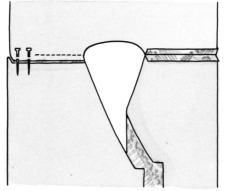

4 Join kimono back to both fronts at shoulder seams, right sides together. Starting at the armhole edges, pin, baste and stitch seams. Press seams open. Open pieces to wrong side.

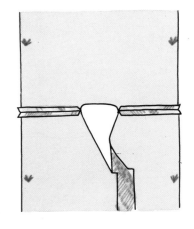

5 To establish the lengths of the armholes, measure 11in (28cm) from the shoulder seams down all four side edges. mark these underarm points with tailor's tacks (see Volume 1, page 52).

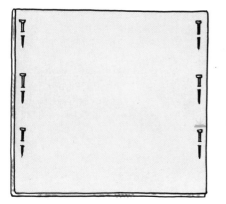

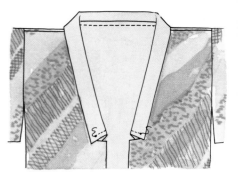

11 Fold band in half lengthwise, right sides together, and stitch both short ends to within ⅝in (1.5cm) of edge.

6 Fold sleeve in half along the crosswise grain of the fabric, to make a square measuring 16⅜in (41.5cm) on each side. Pin raw edges together. Measure 11in (28cm) down from folded edge on one side and mark with a tailor's tack through both layers. Pull layers apart gently and snip tacks so that both sides of sleeve are marked. Remove pins and open sleeve out. Repeat for other sleeve.

8 With right sides together and raw edges level, pin, baste and stitch sleeve seam starting at underarm point. Stitch to ⅝in (1.5cm) from sleeve lower edge; with needle down, pivot fabric 90 degrees. Continue stitching the seam to the sleeve edge. Snip off the seam allowance across the corner. Press seams open. Repeat for other sleeve.

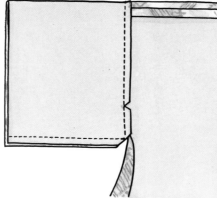

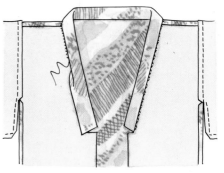

12 Turn band right side out and press. Turn under seam allowance along raw edge and slip stitch to the inside of the kimono.

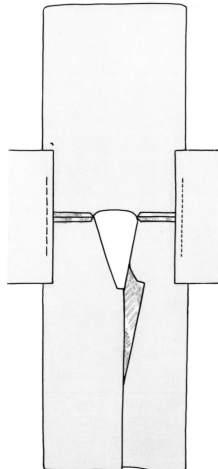

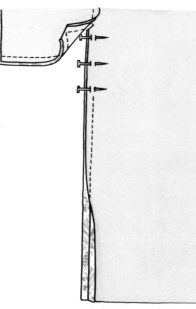

9 Pin, baste and stitch kimono side seams (checking that raw edges are even) from underarm point to hem edge.

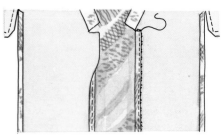

13 Machine finish raw edges of fronts. Fold these edges to inside of kimono so that the folded edge is even with the neckband seam. Hem by hand.

7 With right sides together, raw edges even and tailor's tacks matching on kimono body and sleeve, pin, baste and stitch sleeves to armhole edge between tailor's tacks. Clip seam allowance at underarm points. Press seams together towards kimono body. Repeat for other side.

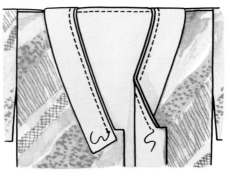

10 With right sides together, raw edges even and centers matching, pin, baste and stitch one long edge of neckband to kimono, finishing stitching ⅝in (1.5cm) from each end of band. Press seam toward band.

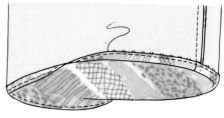

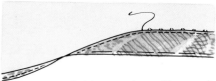

14 Machine finish raw edges of hem and sleeves. Try on kimono to check length. Turn up sleeve and lower edge by the desired amount. Baste and hem by hand.

Terry Evans

104

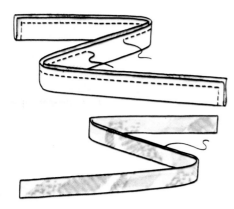

15 Fold belt in half lengthwise, right sides together and raw edges even. Pin, baste and stitch, leaving 4in (10cm) opening in the center of one long edge for turning through. Trim seam allowances and turn belt right side out. Slip stitch opening. Press.

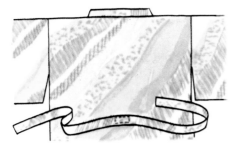

16 Pin center of belt to kimono back, on right side, 15¾in (40cm) below center back neck. Try on kimono and check that belt is correctly positioned. Topstitch a rectangle 2 × 4in (5×10cm) to secure in place as shown.

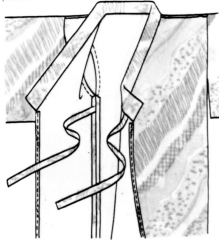

17 If you want to add inner ties, cut tape or seam binding in half. Stitch one half to the inside right-hand seam and the other half to the left center front, both at belt level.

Man's kimono

Measurements (to fit chest sizes 36–46in [92—177cm]).
Finished length, 35¼in (89.5cm).
Hem and seam allowances are the same as for the woman's version.

Materials
2¼yd (2m) of 36in (90cm)-wide solid-color fabric
2½yd (2.2m) of 36in (90cm)-wide stiped fabric
Scrap of fabric for the motif (the fabric should be closely woven)
Notions as for woman's version

1 Following measurement diagram for man's version, cut a rectangle for the back from solid-color fabric and cut out neck curve as instructed for woman's version. For side fronts, cut two rectangles from solid fabric. For center front panels, cut two rectangles from stiped fabric. Cut two sleeves and two strips for neckband from the striped fabric. Cut belt from solid fabric. Following appropriate measurements, cut front shaping (see woman's version).

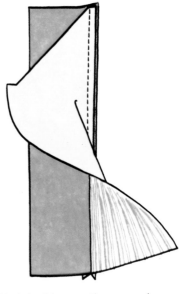

2 With right sides together, raw edges even, pin, baste, and stitch striped center front panel to solid side panel. Press seam open. Repeat for other side. Join shoulder seams.

Terry Evans

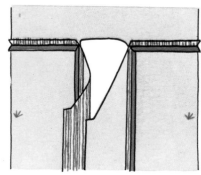

3 To establish length of armholes measure 13in (33cm) down each side edge of shoulder seams. Mark with tailor's tacks as for woman's version.

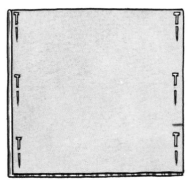

4 Fold each striped sleeve piece in half to make a square and pin edges together. Measure 13in (33cm) down from fold and mark.

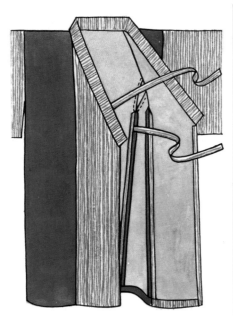

5 Complete kimono as for woman's version with the following exceptions: Join the two neckband strips with ⅝in (1.5cm) seam allowances. Attach one inner tape inside left side seam and other to right center front. Attach belt 17¾in (45cm) below center back neck. Trim kimono with appliqué motif.

Herb Schmitz

Technique tip

Appliquéd motif

On a sheet of paper, draw the name or initials freehand to the correct size. Graph paper will help you to get the proportions correct; see page 110 for instructions for enlarging a design on graph paper.
Next, iron a piece of interfacing to the wrong side of the fabric. This will prevent the raw edges from fraying.
Place the paper letters on the right side of the faced fabric. Fix them in position with small pieces of transparent tape, and carefully draw around the outlines with pencil or chalk, as close to the paper edges as possible. Remove paper pattern; join the lines along the gaps made by the tape. Cut

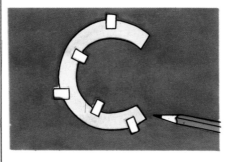

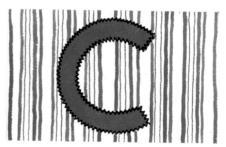

out the letters from the fabric. Pin and baste them to the kimono front. Stitch in place with satin stitch (close zig-zag), taking care to pivot the needle at sharp angles, or stitch by hand, using buttonhole stitch. (See Sewing Course 8, page 51).

Needlework

Cool and comfortable pillows

Machine or hand appliqué is an easy way to make a plain pillow into something very special. Look around you for ideas for your own designs . . . these lovely patterns were inspired by some Japanese prints. We give directions for making the pink pillow.

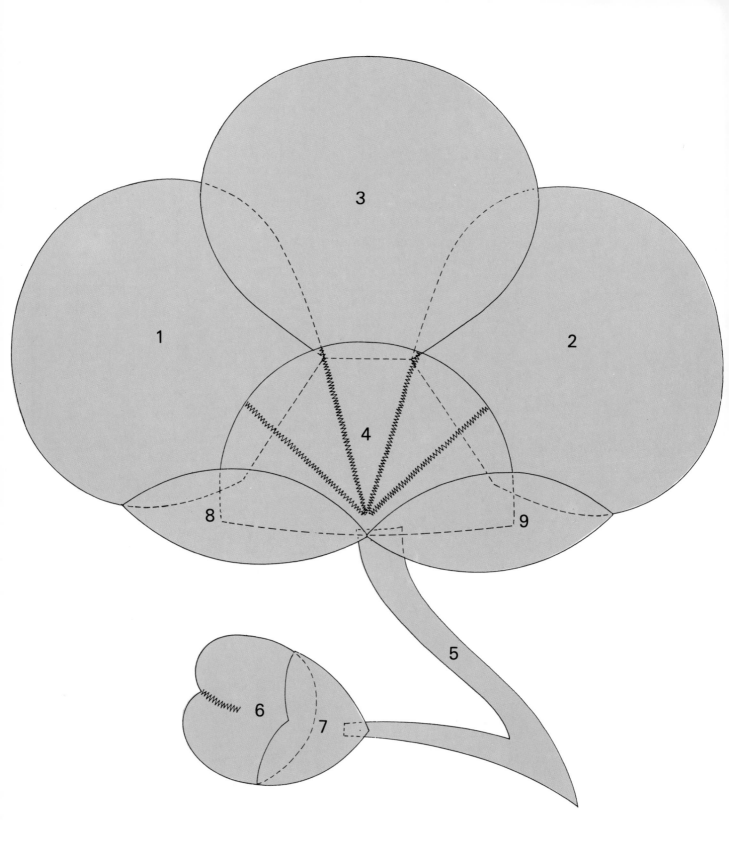

Note: The numbers represent the order in which the pieces should be applied. The dotted lines indicate the areas where the pieces overlap. The zig-zag lines indicate machine zig-zag or hand embroidery.

Materials (for 1 pillow)
⅝yd (.5m) of 36in (90cm)-wide solid color fabric
16in (40cm) square of cotton print fabric for border
Scraps of solid and printed cottons for motifs
Iron-on interfacing
matching sewing thread

16in (40cm) square pillow form
10in (25cm) zipper (optional)
Dressmaker's carbon paper

Note: We recommend the use of iron-on or fusible interfacing to apply the motif, to prevent the edges from raveling.

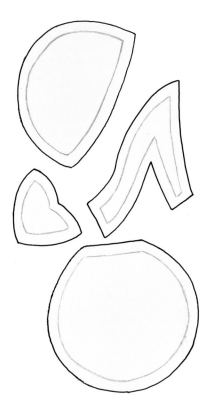

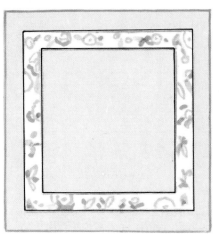

3 Cut out two 18in (45cm) squares from the pink fabric for back and front of cover.
4 With right sides up, position border on cover front with outer edge of border 2in (5cm) from raw edges. Secure in position with basting.

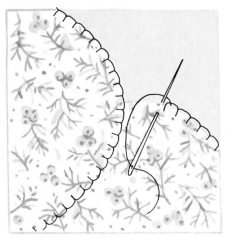

7 Use blanket stitch if you are working by hand.

1 Trace the motifs from the pattern and transfer to the interfacing with the carbon paper. Draw a border 1⅜in (3.5cm) wide and 13in (33cm) long on the outside edges, on the interfacing. Cut out motifs and border, leaving an extra ¼in (5mm) around all edges. (The dotted lines on the diagram indicate where parts of the design overlap.)

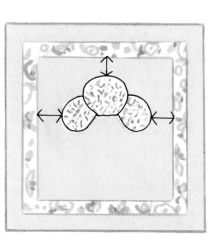

5 Position the flower pieces in the order indicated on the pattern in the center of of the border.

8 machine embroider where indicated, using either zig-zag or satin stitch.

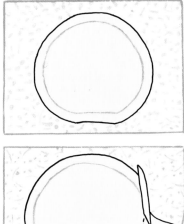

2 Iron each motif and the border on the back of the appropriate fabrics. Allow to cool, then cut out accurately around each shape, trimming off the ¼in (5mm) border.

6 Using matching thread, stitch around the edge of each appliqué piece using close machine zig-zag stitch.

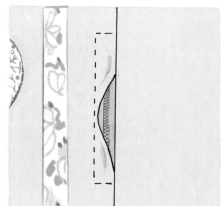

9 If using a zipper, insert this into the center of one side seam.

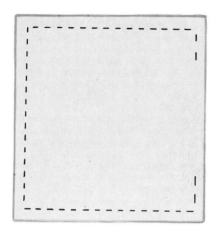

10 Place back of cover on front with right sides together, raw edges even. Stitch together, taking 1in (2.5cm) seams and leaving 10in (25cm) opening for turning out.

11 Turn cover right side out. Insert pillow form and slip stitch the opening closed, if you have not fitted a zipper.

Enlarging a motif

These motifs for the other two appliquéd pillows can easily be enlarged to any size you like. As shown, they are less than one fourth of the actual size—each square on the grid represents a square measuring 1in (2.5cm) on each side.

Use a sheet of graph paper, or, using a ruler, draw a grid of 1in (2.5cm) squares, 21 across and 21 down on a sheet of plain paper. Copy the motifs on the enlarged grid, positioning each part of the drawing on the square corresponding to the equivalent square on the small grid.

This technique can be used to enlarge or reduce a design to any desired size. For example, if you want to reduce a design by half, draw a grid over the original, then draw a grid containing the same number of squares, half the size, and copy the design on it.

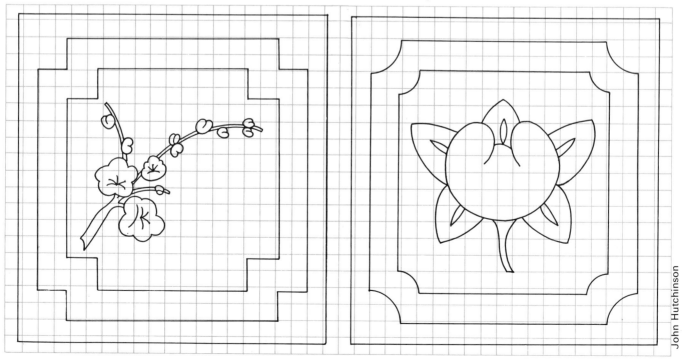

John Hutchinson

Make your own bouquets garnis to enhance your cooking and store them in this clear plastic holder which hangs on the kitchen wall.

Bouquets for the cook

Materials

One piece of clear plastic $12\frac{1}{2} \times 11$in (32×28cm)
One piece of gingham $6\frac{1}{4} \times 11$in (16×28cm)
$1\frac{1}{8}$yd (1m) of $\frac{1}{2}$in (1.3cm)-wide bias binding
$\frac{5}{8}$yd (.5m) of 36in (90cm)-wide cheesecloth
Sprigs of thyme, sage and bay leaves or $\frac{1}{2}$oz (15g) of each herb, dried
Piece of paper 16in (40cm) square
Thread, transparent tape, compass

Bouquets garnis

1 Cut out forty 4in (10cm) squares of cheesecloth.
2 Use the squares double for each bouquet garni. Lay two squares together, matching all edges. Put a sprig or small pinch of each herb in the center of the double square.
3 Draw up the fabric around the herbs, bind the edges tightly with red thread, and knot carefully, leaving about 4in (10cm) of thread at each end.
4 Knot the ends of the thread together again, making a loop that will anchor the bouquet garni to the saucepan handle.

Holder

1 For front pattern, on paper draw a rectangle $6\frac{1}{4} \times 7$in(16×18cm). For back pattern, draw an identical rectangle. For the rounded top, on one short edge draw a semi-circle with a radius of 3in (7.5cm), using a compass. Cut out both patterns.
2 Place the front and back pattern on clear plastic, allowing $\frac{3}{8}$in (1cm) between patterns. Draw around each pattern with a ballpoint pen. Cut out the pieces, adding $\frac{1}{4}$in (5mm) all around.
3 Place back pattern on gingham fabric, mark around it and cut out, adding $\frac{1}{4}$in (5mm) all around.
4 Matching right side of gingham to one side of back plastic piece, tape the two pieces together.
5 Stitch across marked line at top of front piece. Cut a strip of binding the length of the top of the front section. Fold binding in half over top of front section and, on each side, slip stitch to the stitches running along the edge of the plastic. Zig-zag in place.
6 Place front plastic piece on unlined side of back section matching sides and base edges. Fasten the layers together with tape. Sew them together around matched edges and continue stitching around top of back piece.
7 Cut a piece of binding long enough to fit all around holder, plus 4in (10cm). Starting at the top of the curved edge,

fold binding in half over the edge of the holder and slip stitch to the stitches running along the edges as in step 5. Turn under raw ends and make a loop at free end of binding. Slip stitch edges.
8 Zig-zag all around the holder.

Kim Saver

Homemaker

The owl and the pussycat

"The owl and the pussycat went to sea in a beautiful pea-green boat . . ." This charming pair of stuffed toys make a marvelous present for children and "young" adults alike. Here we give directions for making the owl; on page 116 we tell how to make the pussycat.

Materials
7/8 yd (.7m) of 36in (90cm)-wide brown corduroy
Brown felt, 12×16in (30×40cm)
White felt, 10×12in (25×30cm)
Orange felt, 10×12in (25×30cm)
Black felt, 4in (10cm) square
Sewing thread to match each color
7/8 yd (.7m) of 1½in (4cm)-wide blue gingham ribbon
Fiberfill
Dressmaker's tracing paper

Caroline Arber

112

1 Trace all the pieces on the appropriate fabrics with the tracing paper, as directed on the pattern key (see over).

2 Face. Position the body feathers on one body piece. Position the white bib and eye rim pieces on top of this. Pin, baste and stitch around the bib and the eye rims close to the edge, securing feathers in place at the same time.

3 Eyes. Pin and stitch black circles in the middle of brown circles. Stitch white cross in position. Pin eyes to rim section and topstitch close to edge of eyes. Pad the eyes slightly to give them a raised effect.

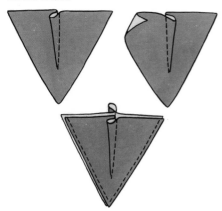

4 Beak. Pin and stitch the two darts, tapering the stitching toward the points to form a ridge on the outside of the beak. Pin the two beak pieces together and stitch close to edge along sides. Stuff beak. Pin in position on the face. Sew securely in place.

5 Wings. Place feather strip along lower curved edge of wing on right side of fabric. Pin and baste in position before placing wing pieces right sides together. Stitch along curved edges close to seamline. Turn right side out and top-stitch close to seamline. Stuff and stitch across open end to hold filling in place.

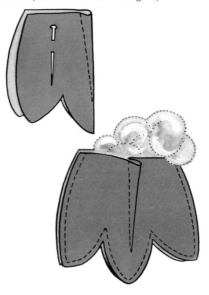

6 Feet. Fold two claw pieces in half with right sides outside. Stitch a narrow line along fold, tapering toward the point of the central claw. With wrong sides facing, pin these upper claw pieces to the lower pieces. Stitch close to edge around claws, leaving straight edge open. Stuff and stitch along open edge to hold stuffing in place.

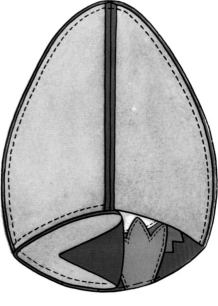

Terry Evans

7 Body. Pin wings in correct position on seamlines as indicated on pattern for front body. With right sides together, pin, baste and stitch the body seamlines together, making sure they meet neatly and accurately at top of body.
Similarly pin and baste the feet in position on the base seamline of the front body piece. With right sides together, matching the "corners" of the base with the body seamlines, pin, baste and stitch the base, leaving an opening to turn through. Turn right side out and stuff firmly, making sure all the curves, particularly along seams, are well packed and shaped, and sew opening by hand.

8 Bow. Tie a bow, using the gingham ribbon and sew it securely on bib.

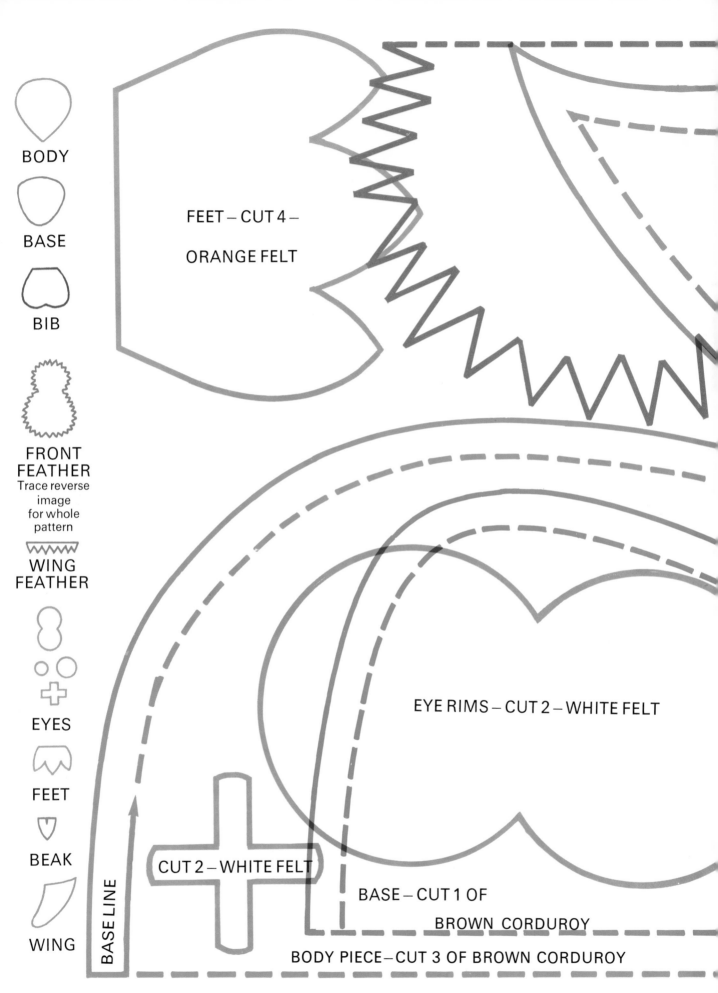

BODY

BASE

BIB

FRONT
FEATHER
Trace reverse
image
for whole
pattern

WING
FEATHER

EYES

FEET

BEAK

WING

FEET – CUT 4 –

ORANGE FELT

EYE RIMS – CUT 2 – WHITE FELT

BASE LINE

CUT 2 – WHITE FELT

BASE – CUT 1 OF

BROWN CORDUROY

BODY PIECE – CUT 3 OF BROWN CORDUROY

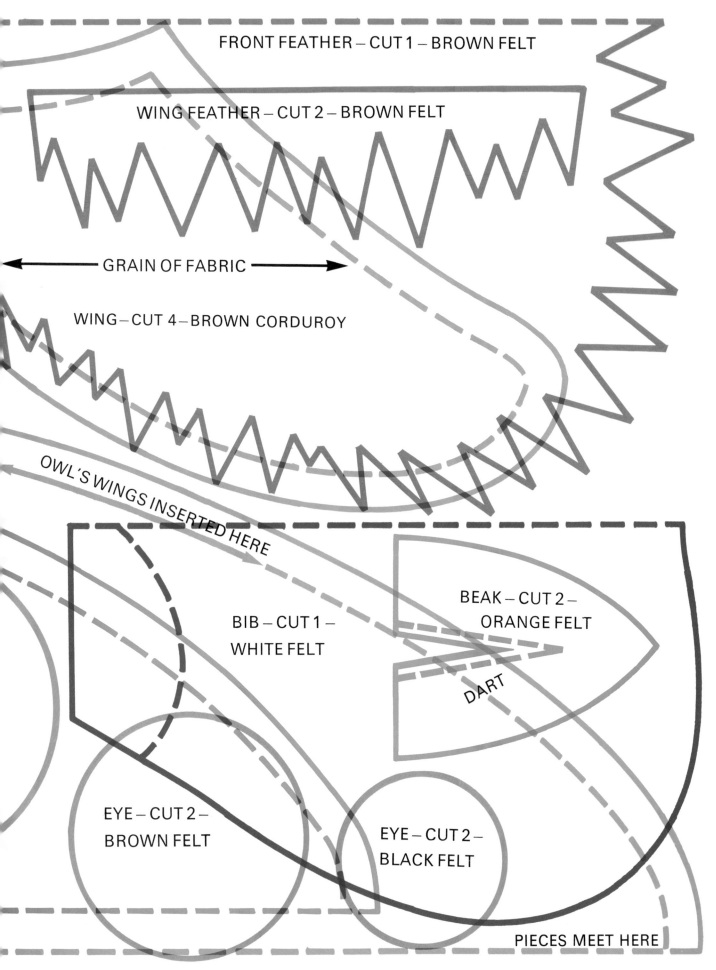

FRONT FEATHER – CUT 1 – BROWN FELT

WING FEATHER – CUT 2 – BROWN FELT

← GRAIN OF FABRIC →

WING – CUT 4 – BROWN CORDUROY

OWL'S WINGS INSERTED HERE

BIB – CUT 1 – WHITE FELT

BEAK – CUT 2 – ORANGE FELT

DART

EYE – CUT 2 – BROWN FELT

EYE – CUT 2 – BLACK FELT

PIECES MEET HERE

Homemaker

The owl and the pussycat (2)

"What a beautiful pussy you are . . ." So said the Owl to his furry friend as they sailed away in their pea-green boat. Make this charming pussycat as a companion for the owl (directions for the owl were given on page 112), and delight a small friend of your own.

Trace all the pieces on tracing paper: then transfer to the appropriate fabrics using the carbon paper.

2 Eyes. Topstitch the green pieces on the white and then the black pupils centrally on the green. Using white embroidery floss, hand embroider a small block of the pupils with about four straight stitches to give a "twinkle" to each eye. Pin and stitch eyes to the body piece.

Materials

$\frac{7}{8}$yd (.7m) of 36in (90cm)-wide black corduroy
White felt, 10×12in (25×30cm)
Pink felt, 10×12in (25×30cm)
Green felt, 4in (10cm) square
Scraps of black felt
Sewing thread to match each color
1 skein white cotton embroidery floss
$\frac{7}{8}$yd (.7m) of 1½in (4cm)-wide green gingham ribbon
1$\frac{5}{8}$yd (1.5m) fine string for whiskers
Starch or fabric stiffener for whiskers
Stuffing
Large-eyed needle
Tracing paper
Dressmaker's carbon paper
Pencil

Face. Pin and topstitch the white bib in position. Topstitch the two tongue pieces together, keeping close to the edge. Pin this in position on the body, as shown. Place the cheeks over the upper edge of the tongue and pad slightly with stuffing while stitching.

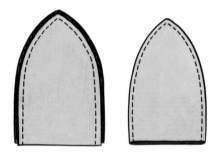

3 Ears. With rights sides together, pin and baste one felt and one corduroy piece together. Stitch along seamlines, leaving straight edge open. Turn right side out and topstitch along edge using the appropriate colored thread. Fold over one edge of each ear and baste along seamline to give shape to ear. Remember to make a right and left ear.

4 Feet. With right sides together, pin and stitch along seamlines, leaving straight edge open. Turn right side out and stuff. Stitch along opening to hold stuffing in place. With white embroidery floss, embroider four claws on each foot, using straight stitch.

5 Tail. With right sides together, pin and stitch the straight edge of the white tail tip to the black corduroy strip. Press seam open. Fold tail in half lengthwise and stitch along seamline. Leave short, straight end open. Turn right side out and stuff. Stitch across open end to hold stuffing in place.

7 Whiskers. Using fabric stiffener coat the narrow string several times until it is fairly rigid. Cut eight pieces approximately 4in (10cm) long and eight pieces 3in (8cm) long. Thread four 4in (10cm) pieces through each cheek and four 3in (8cm) pieces above each eye, using a large needle. Tie a knot on each side of the fabric to hold the string whiskers firmly in position.

8 Stuffing. Stuff body firmly and hand stitch opening to close.
9 Bow. Tie a bow using a gingham ribbon and hand stitch securely in place on bib.

Terry Evans

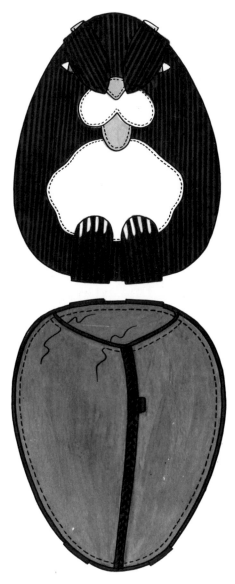

6 Body. Pin and baste ears in position on "head". Pin and baste feet in position along base seamline of body front. With right sides together, join side seams and back seam, inserting tail at base of back seam. With right sides together, matching the "corners" of the base with the body seamlines, pin, baste and stitch the base, leaving an opening. Turn right side out.

Caroline Arber

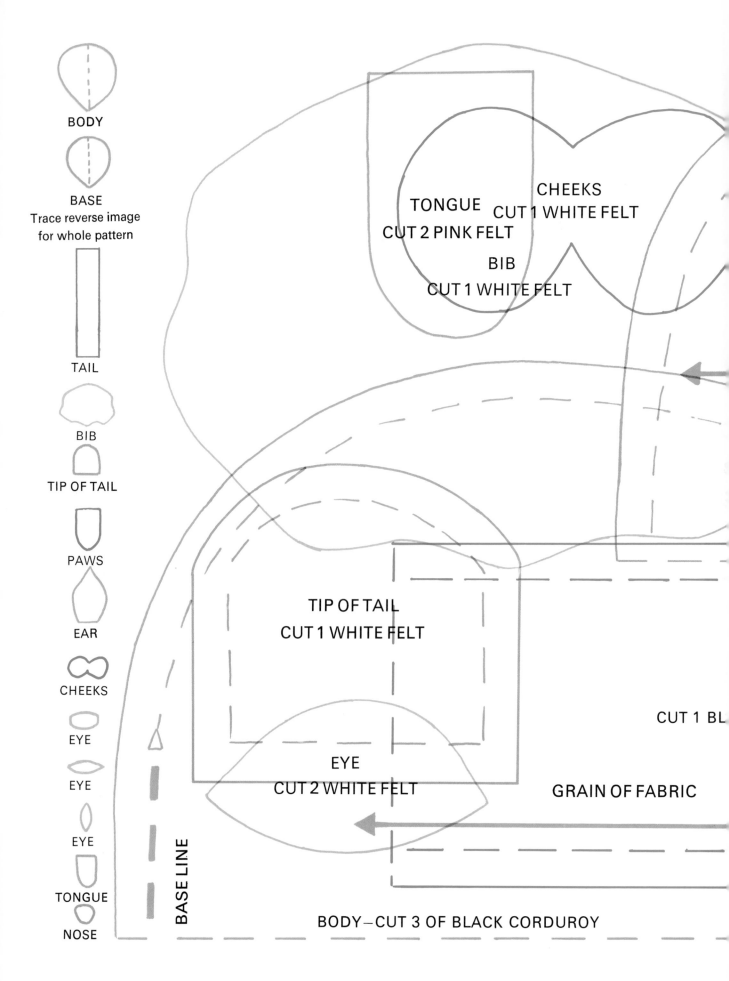

BODY

BASE
Trace reverse image
for whole pattern

TAIL

BIB

TIP OF TAIL

PAWS

EAR

CHEEKS

EYE

EYE

EYE

TONGUE

NOSE

BASE LINE

TONGUE
CUT 2 PINK FELT

CHEEKS
CUT 1 WHITE FELT

BIB
CUT 1 WHITE FELT

TIP OF TAIL
CUT 1 WHITE FELT

CUT 1 BL

EYE
CUT 2 WHITE FELT

GRAIN OF FABRIC

BODY–CUT 3 OF BLACK CORDUROY

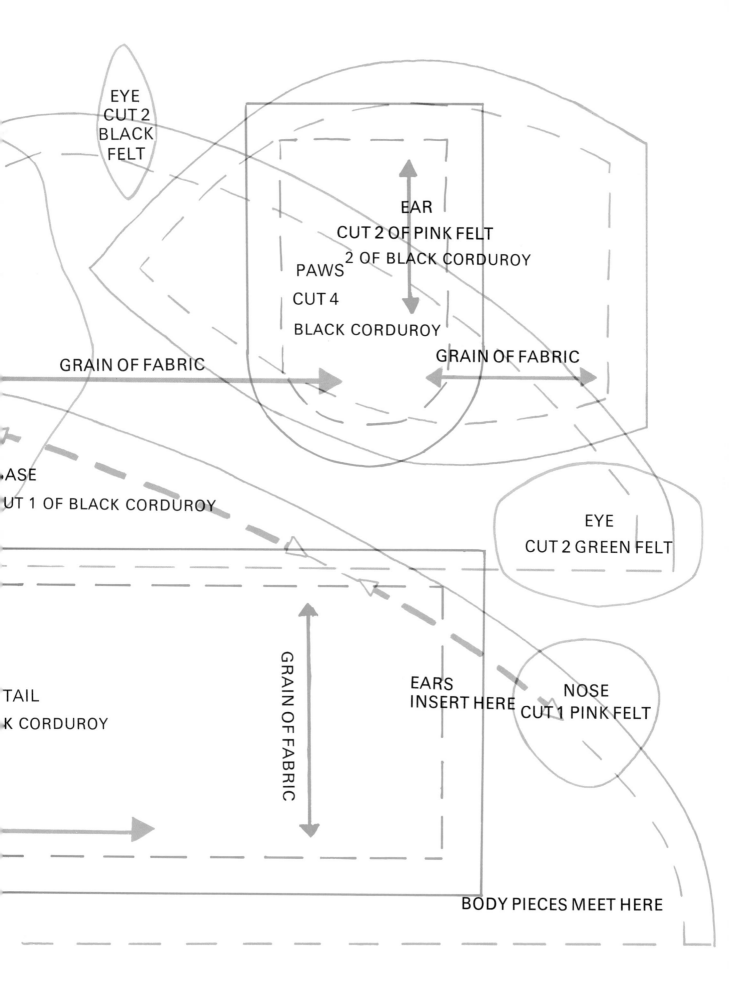

EYE
CUT 2
BLACK
FELT

EAR
CUT 2 OF PINK FELT
2 OF BLACK CORDUROY

PAWS
CUT 4
BLACK CORDUROY

GRAIN OF FABRIC

GRAIN OF FABRIC

ASE
UT 1 OF BLACK CORDUROY

EYE
CUT 2 GREEN FELT

GRAIN OF FABRIC

TAIL
K CORDUROY

EARS
INSERT HERE

NOSE
CUT 1 PINK FELT

BODY PIECES MEET HERE

Homemaker

In the Round

A set of co-ordinated tablecloths in fresh country fabric can brighten up a room or give an old table a new lease of life. The ruffled floor-length cloth is covered with a short cloth in a pretty flower print. Both are edged with bias binding.

Plain circular tablecloth

Calculating the fabric
Measure the diameter of the table, then decide how much overhang you want. For a short cloth, measure from the top of the table to a chair seat; for a long overhang, measure to the floor. Multiply this overhang by two and add this to the diameter of the table. This will give you the diameter of the finished tablecloth. If the diameter is less than the width of your selected fabric, one length of fabric will be enough. However, if the diameter is wider, you will need to join two or more lengths of fabric. If the fabric has a large design, also allow one extra pattern repeat per extra length of fabric for matching.

Materials
For a tablecloth 2yd (1.8m) in diameter
  4yd (3.7m)×48in (122cm)-wide fabric
    (if the fabric has a large design, add
    one extra pattern repeat)
  6½yd (6m) bias binding for edging
    (or ½yd (50cm) solid fabric)
  Matching sewing thread
  Paper for pattern
  Pencil and string

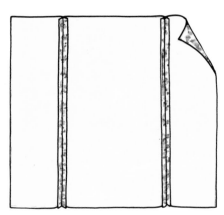

1 Starting with a straight edge, cut one length of fabric the same length as the diameter of the finished tablecloth. Cut the remaining fabric in half lengthwise. Join one strip to each side of the first

length, taking a ⅝in (1.5cm)-wide seam allowance and matching the pattern carefully; pin, baste and stitch. Cut the strips even with the first length of fabric. Trim seam allowances to ⅜in (1cm) and finish the raw edges.

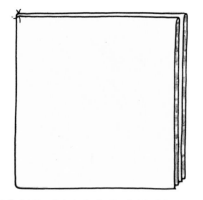

2 Fold the fabric in half, right sides together, and then fold it in half again. Mark the corner which is the center of the fabric with a tailor's tack.

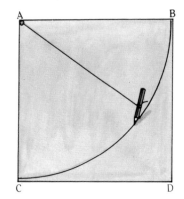

3 Cut a square of paper the same size as the folded fabric. Tie one end of a piece of string around a pin and the other end around a pencil; the distance between the pin and the pencil should equal the radius of the tablecloth. Put the pin at corner A of the paper square and, holding the pencil at a right angle to the paper, draw an arc from corner B to corner C. Cut out the pattern.

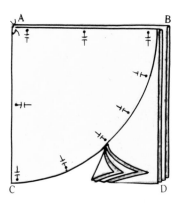

4 Place the pattern on the folded fabric so that corner A is on top of the tailor's tack. Pin and cut out along the curved line of the pattern from C to B.

5 Unpin the pattern and unfold the fabric. Stitch bias binding to the edge of the cloth.

Floor-length tablecloth with ruffle

Calculating the fabric
Measure the diameter of the table. Add ¾in (2cm) to this meaurement for seam allowances. This is the diameter of the top piece and equals the length of fabric required. However, if your table is wider than the fabric, you will need two lengths plus one extra pattern repeat for matching the design.
Measure the distance from the table top to the floor and add ⅜in (1cm) for the seam allowance. This is the total depth of the ruffle and should be cut from the width of the fabric.
To calculate the length of fabric required for the ruffle, measure the circumference of the table. For a full ruffle, allow twice this measurement. If less fullness is required, 1½ times is sufficient. Also add 1⅛in (3cm) for seam allowances. This measurement will also give you the required length of bias binding for the bottom edge.

Size 48in (120cm) in diameter with a full 30in (75cm) deep ruffle.

Materials

  10½yd (9.6m)×48in (122cm)-wide
    fabric
  9¼yd (8.5m) bias binding for edging
    (or ½yd (50cm) plain fabric)
  Matching sewing thread
  Paper for pattern

1 Cut out the circular piece for the tablecloth as for the short cloth. (Unless your table is wider than 48in (120cm), you will not need to join lengths of fabric.) Cut the ruffle, then cut along one side of the fabric to get the correct depth.

2 With right sides together, pin, baste and stitch the short sides of the ruffle, taking a ⅝in (1.5cm)-wide seam allowance. Finish the raw edges and press the seam open. Using the longest stitch on the sewing machine, run a double row of stitching ⅜in (1cm) from the top edge of the ruffle. Carefully pull up the bobbin threads of the two gathering rows until the ruffle is the right size. At the ends of the gathering lines, wind the threads around a pin in a figure eight to make the final adjustment of the gathers easier.

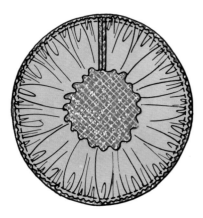

3 With right sides together and raw edges matching, pin the ruffle to the top piece, making sure that the gathers are evenly

Technique tip

Bias binding

Bias binding is used to finish raw edges and produce a decorative finish. It can be made from the same fabric as the main article, or in a matching or contrasting solid fabric. The advantage of bias binding is that it can stretch and go around curves without puckering.

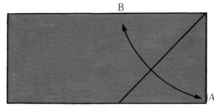

Cutting bias strips
To find the bias grain, fold the fabric so that one selvage is at a right angle to the other selvage (from A to B).

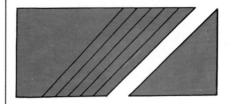

Cut along the fold line and cut 1in (2.5cm) strips parallel to the first cutting line. 1in (2.5cm) is wide enough for most purposes, but cording, for example, may require slightly wider strips.

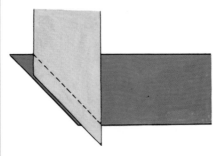

Joining strips
Place the strips with right sides together and raw edges matching. Pin, baste and stitch ⅜in (1cm) from the edge. Unfold the strip, press the seam open and trim the corners.

spaced. Baste carefully and stitch ⅜in (1cm) from the edge. Remove the basting and press the seam allowances toward

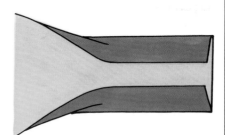

Folding the binding
Turn under ¼in (5mm) to the wrong side along each edge and press well.

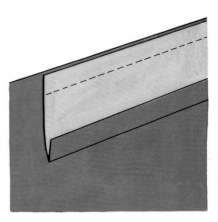

Applying binding
Unfold one edge of the binding and place it along the raw edge of the fabric, right sides together and raw edges matching. Pin in position. Baste and stitch along the fold line.

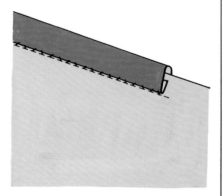

Fold the binding over to the wrong side of the fabric. Slip-stitch along the original seamline, or machine stitch very close to the edge.

the top piece, trim and finish raw edges. Finish the edge of the ruffle with bias binding as for the short cloth.

Terry Evans

Homemaker

Pajama case clown

Sometimes he's happy, sometimes he's blue. But whichever way you turn him, he's useful — keeping a child's pajamas neatly tucked away 'till bedtime.

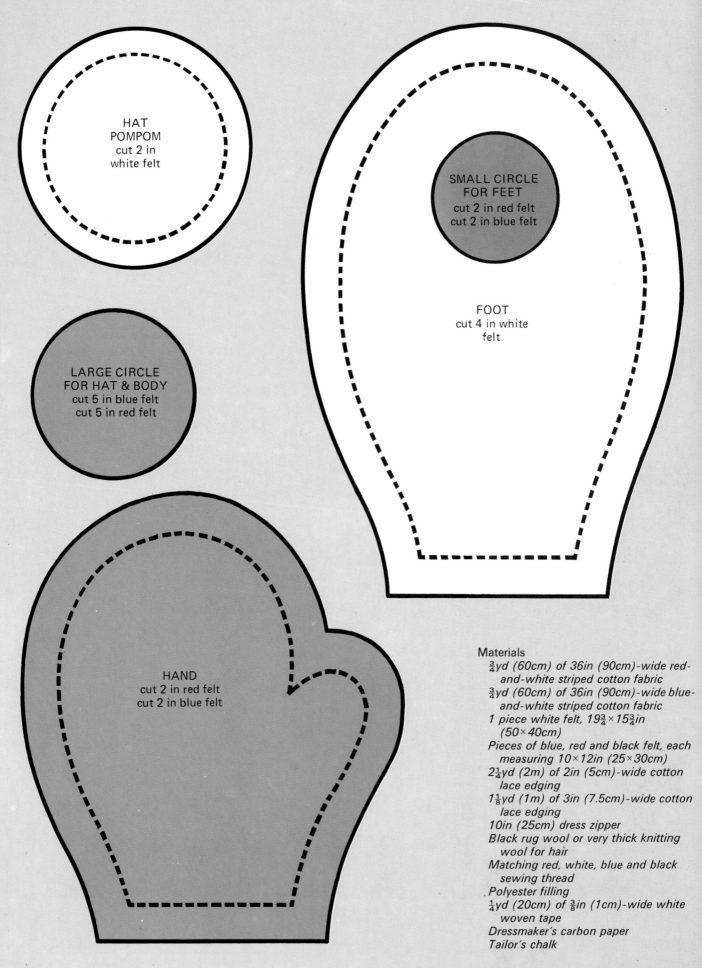

HAT
POMPOM
cut 2 in
white felt

SMALL CIRCLE
FOR FEET
cut 2 in red felt
cut 2 in blue felt

FOOT
cut 4 in white
felt

LARGE CIRCLE
FOR HAT & BODY
cut 5 in blue felt
cut 5 in red felt

HAND
cut 2 in red felt
cut 2 in blue felt

Materials

¾yd (60cm) of 36in (90cm)-wide red-
and-white striped cotton fabric
¾yd (60cm) of 36in (90cm)-wide blue-
and-white striped cotton fabric
1 piece white felt, 19¾×15¾in
(50×40cm)
Pieces of blue, red and black felt, each
measuring 10×12in (25×30cm)
2¼yd (2m) of 2in (5cm)-wide cotton
lace edging
1⅛yd (1m) of 3in (7.5cm)-wide cotton
lace edging
10in (25cm) dress zipper
Black rug wool or very thick knitting
wool for hair
Matching red, white, blue and black
sewing thread
Polyester filling
¼yd (20cm) of ⅜in (1cm)-wide white
woven tape
Dressmaker's carbon paper
Tailor's chalk

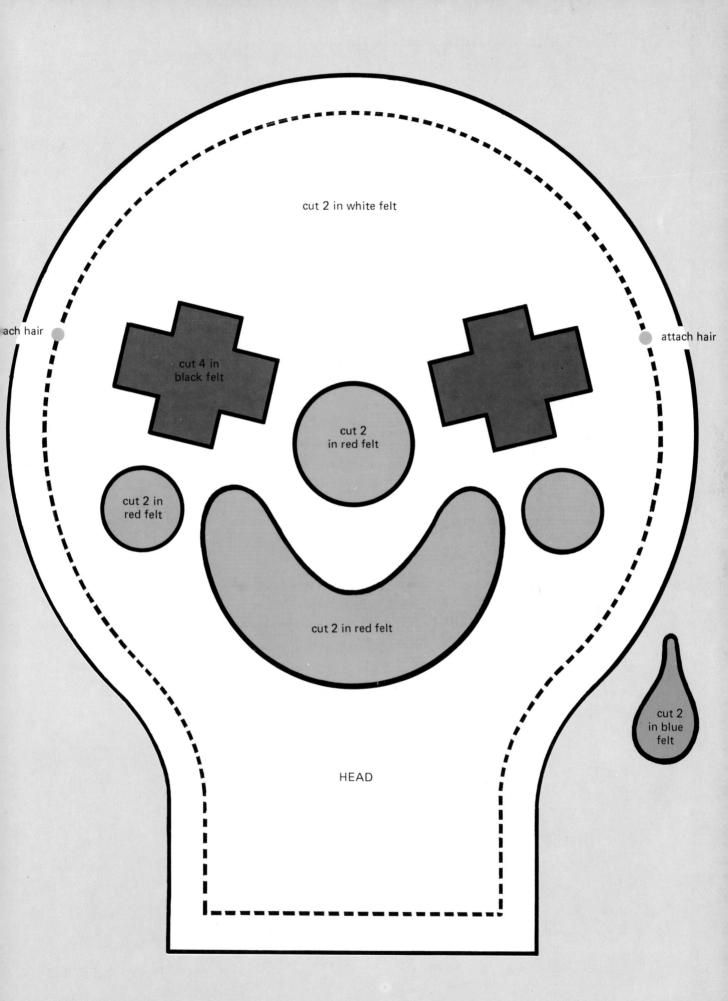

cut 2 in white felt

attach hair

attach hair

cut 4 in
black felt

cut 2
in red felt

cut 2 in
red felt

cut 2 in red felt

cut 2
in blue
felt

HEAD

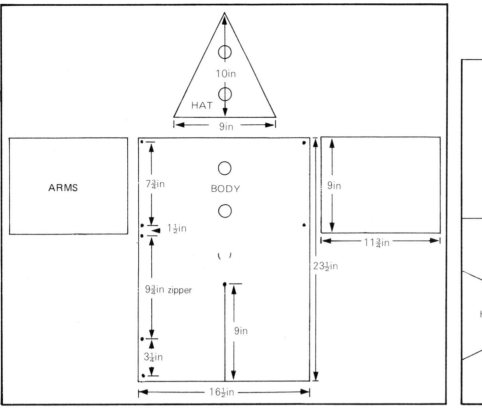

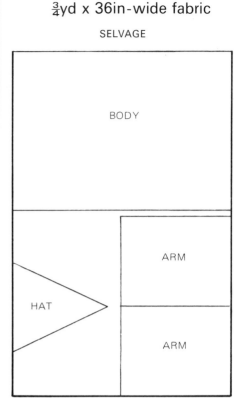

1 Following the measurements given in the diagram for the main body piece, draw a rectangle on the red-striped fabric with tailor's chalk. Mark in the positions of the zipper, the legs, the arms and the three felt circles. Cut out the rectangle. Repeat this on the blue-striped fabric.
For the arms, cut out four rectangles, each measuring 9 × 11$\frac{3}{4}$in (23 × 30cm), two in the red fabric and two in the blue fabric. From the remaining pieces of striped fabric cut out two triangles for the hat, one in each color. Follow the measurements in our diagram, making sure that the stripes run vertically.

2 Trace the head, feet, hands and features on tracing paper and then—using the dressmaker's tracing paper—on to the appropriate colored felts. Cut out the shapes.

3 Pin and baste the features on the two head pieces in their correct positions, as shown. Topstitch close to the edges of the features. Press on wrong side.

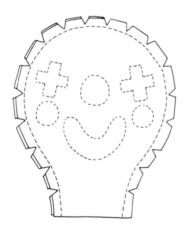

4 With right sides together, pin and stitch the two head pieces around the curved edge, leaving the straight neck edge open. Clip the stitched, curved edge. Turn to right side, stuff with filling. Stitch across neck edges to close.

5 Cut the wool into 24 12in (30cm) lengths and divide it into two equal bunches. Tie each bunch securely in the middle. Hand stitch one bunch firmly in position on each side of the head.

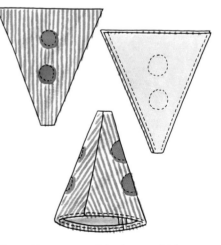

6 Pin and baste two of the large red felt

circles in position on the blue hat piece, and two large blue felt circles in position on the red hat piece. Topstitch close to the edge of the felt pieces. With right sides together pin, baste and stitch the side seams of the hat pieces, taking a ⅝in (1.5cm) seam allowance. Turn right side out; press seams flat. Turn under ⅝in (1.5cm) along the open raw edge, press and work a line of gathering stitches close to folded edge.

leaving a small opening opposite the tape. Turn the felt pompom right side out and stuff softly. Turn the edge of the opening inward to complete finished circle and slip the point of the hat into the opening. Hand stitch the hat firmly in place, closing the pompom opening at the same time.

Stuff and stitch along open edge. Remember there should be a red circle and a blue circle on each foot. Repeat for the other foot.

7 Pin the hat on the head, matching hat and head seams, just above the 'hair' bunches. Draw up gathering threads on hat to fit head; hand stitch the gathered edge neatly to the head, using white thread and stitching through white stipes only.

9 Pin and baste one red and one blue hand piece together to form left hand. Stitch along the seamlines, leaving the wrist edge open. Clip the seam allowance, turn right side out and stuff. Stitch open edge closed. For the right hand, reverse the other two hand pieces, then stitch and stuff in the same way as for the left hand. Make sure you have a right and a left hand.

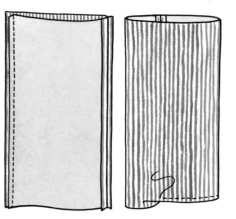

11 Pin and baste one red arm piece and one blue arm piece together along the side seams taking a ⅝in (1.5cm) seam allowance. Stitch seams and press open. Turn right side out. Repeat for other arm. At one end of each arm turn under ⅝in (1.5cm) and press. Measure and cut a length of the narrow lace to fit each arm, allowing a light extra for seams.

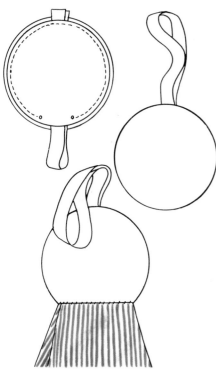

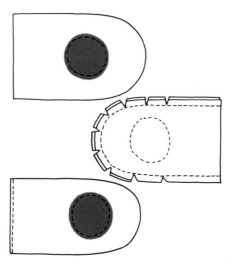

10 Pin and baste the red and blue circles to each of the four foot pieces, one circle on each foot. Topstitch in place close to the edge of the circle. With right sides together, pin and baste two feet pieces along the curved edge. Stitch seams, leaving straight edges open. Clip seam allowances and turn right side out.

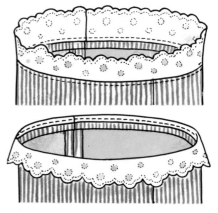

12 Pin and stitch the raw edge of one length of the lace, wrong side up, to the turned-under edge of one of the arms. Fold the edging back over the arm edge

8 Fold the tape in half and place the raw ends between the two white felt circles for the pompom. Pin and stitch around the edge incorporating the tape,

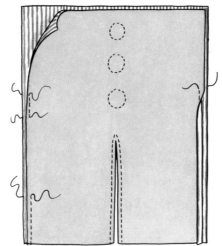

14 Pin and baste the three blue circles to the red body piece, positioning them according to the diagram. Topstitch in place. Repeat for the red circles and blue body piece.

and pin in place. Work a line of gathering stitches close to the folded edge, stitching through both the lace and the sleeve edge. Draw up the gathering tightly, but gently, to prevent gathering thread from breaking.

15 With right sides together, pin and baste the two body pieces together below positions marked for arms and omitting neck edge and lower leg edges. Insert the zipper in the position indicated on the diagram.

17 Finish the neck edge by turning under a $\frac{5}{8}$in (1.5cm) hem; baste and press. Measure and cut a length of the wide lace edging to fit the neck, with a little extra for a seam. Attach the lace in the same way as for the cuffs and gather the neck edge tightly to fit head. Hand sew body firmly to head.

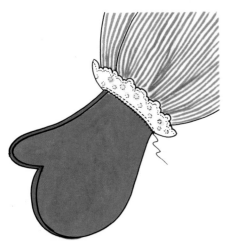

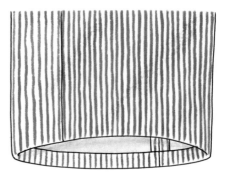

13 Place the hand in the sleeve opening and pin in place. Remember to match the hand and sleeve colors.
Carefully hand stitch the hand to the cuff. Repeat for the other arm and hand.

16 machine stitch the remaining basted edges. Turn under the seam allowances of armholes, baste and press. Pin and baste arms in place just under folded armhole edges, matching colors on both sides. Topstitch the sleeves to the body.

18 Finish each leg edge by turning under a $\frac{5}{8}$in (1.5cm) hem. Trim with narrow lace edging and gather to fit feet. Insert feet and hand stitch securely in place.

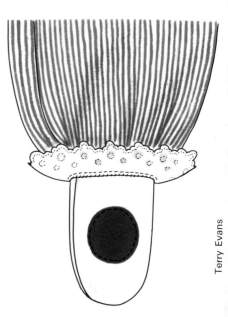

Terry Evans